Lessons Learned from Fire-Rescue Leaders

Insights for Every Leader!

Other Books By Stephen M. Gower, CSP Include:

What Do They See When They See You Coming?
The Power of Perception over Reality

Think Like a Giraffe!
A Reach for the Sky Guide in Creativity and Maximum Performance

Mountains of Motivation!
How to Motivate Yourself and Create a Motivational Environment for Others

The Art of Killing Kudzu
Management By Encouragement

Have You Encouraged Someone Today?
366 Ways to Practice Encouragement

Leadership Re-Think!
How to Claim and Polish the Leader within You

Perception:
Make It Your Business

Traveling By Detour
Living with Struggle and Surprise

Lessons Learned from Fire-Rescue Leaders

Insights for Every Leader!

They Lead in a Challenging World!

Learn from Them!

Stephen M. Gower, CSP
with John M. Buckman, III

LESSONS LEARNED FROM FIRE-RESCUE LEADERS

First edition, published 2008 by LECTERN PUBLISHING, P.O. Box 1065, Toccoa, GA 30577. First Printing, 2008.

Library of Congress Catalog Card No.: 2007906223
ISBN: 978-1-880-150-1-07

CONTENTS

Dedication

The wisest choice that I made on this project was my first decision. When I asked Chief John M. Buckman, III to work with me on this project, I struck gold! To join efforts with a Fire-Rescue Leader of this caliber added tremendous credibility to this venture. Therefore, it is with both pride and a deep sense of appreciation, that I dedicate *Lessons Learned from Fire-Rescue Leaders* to a leader of leaders – Chief John M. Buckman, III.

-SMG

Dedicated to Chief John M. Buckman, III

One of the most recognized Fire-Rescue leaders in the country, and arguably in the world –
A man blessed with integrity, passion, insight, and decades of experience –
A friend to legions, and a gentleman serving to all the honors he has received.

Acknowledgement

I would like to thank Stephen Gower and his staff for pushing and pulling me along this project. They have done a tremendous job in organizing the material and bringing this book to the final phase of printing and distribution.

-JMB

"'How awesome' was the thought I had when I heard Stephen M. Gower and John M. Buckman, III were working on this book. Why didn't someone think of this team earlier? This book should be in every fire chief's desk reference. These two stellar individuals working together will fill your leadership toolbox with powerful leadership techniques and proven, effective application."

Al Yancey, Chief
Minooka, IL Fire Prot. Dist.

"I have known John Buckman for eighteen years. He took me by the hand and pulled me into his world where I learned to become a leader. I wish everyone could be like my brother, John Buckman. Stephen Gower came into my life about five years ago when I attended an Executive Fire Officer's Symposium. I feel his presence as a man of honesty. If you want a road-map to your future in leadership, Stephen Gower will provide it."

Fred Windisch, Chief
Ponderosa, TX Fire Department

"Stephen's presentations are riveting in his ability to tell a humorous story. He also shares a helpful message that is brought to the forefront through his personal insights. Our personnel were completely captivated by his message. The lessons in leadership that he imported to us were extremely relevant."

Andrew Bencomo, Deputy Chief
Las Cruces, NM Fire Department

"I have known Chief John Buckman for over twenty-five years. In my opinion, he is one of America's top fire service leaders and visionaries. John has devoted his life work to his God, his family and to the fire service. He has spent literally thousands of hours on the road preaching the "gospel" of fire service leadership and being a "change agent." I have worked with John on dozens of task forces, committees, and commissions. I know first hand how much work and effort he puts into making America's Fire Service better.

John's trademark Stetson hats and Western boots, along with the always being well-dressed, presents a great image of a "Southern Gentleman." I say that with pride. I would highly recommend that all present and future Fire-Rescue leaders purchase this book, and refer to it often. It is written by two of the best leadership gurus in America."

Jack McElfish, Chief
City of Sandy Springs, GA

"Stephen M. Gower is a breath of fresh air for fire and rescue leaders across the county. His insight into leadership is stellar."

Amy Ramon, General Manager
Cy-Fair Volunteer Fire Dept.
Houston, TX

"I have read John Buckman's articles on leadership for years. I knew it was just a matter of time before he would help write a book. You could see his passion for leadership in ever article. John spelled leadership T-I-M-E: 'When you invest time with your followers, you are giving them the most valuable resource you have.'"

Raul A. Angulo, Captain
Seattle, WA Fire Department

"Stephen M. Gower is a powerful, dynamic and memorable speaker with unique approaches to leadership. Chief John M. Buckman, III is an institution in the fire service, known for his knowledge, integrity and candor. A collaboration between these two figures should be a must-read for anyone involved in a position of leadership within the emergency sector."

Mike Macdonald, Editor
National Fire & Rescue magazine

"Stephen M. Gower is as down-to-earth as imaginable. From moment one, you feel as if he is a special friend, blessed with a marvelous insight to leadership."

Chief Mark Burdick
Glendale, AZ Fire and Life Safety

"Well known to the fire service, Buckman has teamed with the "master of re-think" and "perception professional," Stephen M. Gower. This combination produces a work that should be included in the toolbox of every fire and rescue leader. Buckman's in depth knowledge of our industry is coupled with Gower's keen insight into the relationship between perception and leadership. *Lessons Learned from Fire-Rescue Leaders* is a genuine invitation into visionary leadership."

Stephen R. M. Moreno, III
Tarpon Springs, FL Fire Dept.

"Stephen Gower's presentation *What Do They See When They See You Coming?* at the IAFC's 2006 Fire Rescue International in Dallas last year was eye opening, delightful and directly applicable to the Fire and EMS service."

John G. Murphy, EFO
Carrollton, TX Fire Dept.

"Mr. Gower is a great American storyteller. He captivates and inspires those who hear him speak and read his books. Stephen utilizes humor and uncommon insight as he draws from his experiences to connect with Fire-Rescue Leaders."

George Good, Chief
Tolleson, AZ Fire Department

"Stephen is an inspiration to fire service due to his unique approach to leadership techniques."

Linc Cothren, Chief
Heber Springs, AR Fire Department

"John M. Buckman, III, President of IAFC 2001-2001, is an international leader with energy comparable to the 'Energizer Bunny' and technology like 'Inspector Gadget.'"

Ted Arnesty

"Stephen's strengths lie within his vulnerability."

Patrick Laurienti, Batallion Chief
North Washington Fire Protection District,
Denver, CO

"Mr. Gower greatly impressed me with his thorough knowledge of the concept. I was moved with the sincere, genuine manner with which he could convey substantive content and, at the same time, use humor to accentuate major points."

Dr. George A. Hickman
Memorial University of Newfoundland
Newfoundland, Canada

CHAPTER 1

Redefining Leadership

"The time has come to make leadership a true priority in fire service. Our future is at stake each time we enter the fire station. We can no longer live on lip service to leadership."

-Chief Harry R. Carter, Ph.D. (Retired)
Adelphia, N.J. Fire Company

"Spell leadership T-I-M-E: When you invest time with your followers, you are giving them the most valuable resource you have."

-JMB

"Leadership is not what it used to be; leadership will never be what it used to be."

-SMG

****

Leadership has changed!

Select, historical personalities were ahead of their time. Early on, they recognized the full potential of authentic leadership. We can benefit from their insight.

On a broader perspective, for centuries the mainstream perspective of leadership has been flawed. A dominant view of leadership has been weighted down by power, position, and control.

The full potency of leadership has been stifled by an exclusive club-like mentality and mere imposition. Only within the last decade or two have many leaders in general, Fire-Rescue leaders in particular, begun to appreciate leadership from a fresh viewpoint. The traditional fire service leadership view of "I am the officer" is not appropriate today. Officers hold a formal leadership position. In today's fire department, the ability to influence during informal times is critical.

Until recently, leadership has been equated with management. Leadership and management were presented as synonyms for each other. There was no differentiation between a leader and a manager.

Even today, a few authors write in a manner that equates leadership with management. Gratefully, the genre of contemporary authors is in a minority. Many are perceiving that leadership is not what it used to be.

****

"Tradition has held back fire service leaders."

-Chief Patrick Kelly
City of DeLand, FL Fire Dept.

****

A New Tune

There is a new leadership tune that is beginning to be heard and repeated across the country. Many will suggest that some Fire-Rescue leaders are playing major roles in this symphony of redefining leadership. Other Fire-Rescue leaders can benefit from these trend-setters. Lessons can be learned now.

****

Leadership is a matter of intelligence, trustworthiness, humaneness, courage, and discipline. Reliance on intelligence alone results in rebelliousness. Exercise on humaneness alone results in weakness. Fixation on trust results in folly. Dependence on the strength of courage results in violence. Excessive discipline and sternness in command result in cruelty. When one has all five virtues together, each appropriate to its function, then one can be a leader.

-Sun Tzu, *Art of War*

****

Beyond Fire-Rescue, a Broader Perspective

There is more exciting news. Leaders within every discipline can profit from these insights. Leadership within Fire-Rescue is understandably challenging. This crucible of extraordinary leadership-opportunities offers lessons for every leader.

Whether you are now what we will later refer to as "*Uppercase leader*" or a "*lowercase leader*," you can profit from: *Lessons Learned from Fire-Rescue Leaders! Insights for Every Leader.* Whether you are within or without the Fire-Rescue field, you can benefit.

The subsequent chapters in this book are built upon a shift within leadership-thinking. Leadership has more to offer than previous generations of mainstream leaders have suggested. It is unfortunate that they have limited the dividends of leadership to so few.

A redefining of leadership opens doors. It will broaden the thinking of many. It will lead to a much wider leadership-base. The impact will be significant.

A Culture, Not a Club

Lessons Learned from Fire-Rescue Leaders! confirms this cultural shifting. We have learned from our respondents that leadership does not equal an elitist club. Genuine leadership is an embracing culture.

Our surveys indicate a significant leadership rethinking. Leadership is moving from a "narrow-cast" frame of reference to more of a "broadcasting" perspective. The definition of "Who is the leader?" is in a state of flex.

The cultural diversity of fire service has changed. "Diversity" is a new word in the fire service, especially in the area of female and various ethnic backgrounds. Until about 20 years ago, the fire department was primarily staffed with white males. The techniques a leader uses to deal with issues today is significantly different than in the past.

Whereas past leaders have interpreted leadership "selectively," our leader-respondents seem to have a "broader" interpretation of leadership. There is an apparent broader scope of "wiggle room" in defining leaders. Where the focus of the past was "tight," the emphasis from our study approaches "loose."

The Big "I"

The surveys we used to help us garner information for this book revealed a common theme. We asked our respondents to share with us three, one-word synonyms for leadership. We suspected this might be a challenge because only one word could be used for the synonym. We stated as much (the difficulty factor) in our instructions for this question.

The common theme that surfaced was the frequency with which many shared synonyms began with the same letter, "I." Three specific words appeared often: Influence, intuition, inspiration. Issues related to intuition and inspiration will be covered in subsequent chapters. The big "I" is the subject of this segment.

The big "I" is not the first person pronoun. To the contrary, a new model for leadership emphasizes "We, Us, and Our" much more than "I, Me, and Mine."

For purposes of this segment in particular, and the balance of the book in general, the big "I" equals "Influence." A redefined leadership has a nickname. It is Influence.

The respondents indicated a comprehension of leadership that highlights the influence-factor within leaders. They were sensitive to the fact that their influence-clock is always running.

The big "I," Influence, is directly related to our previously stated concept: "If leadership encompasses influence (and it does), then why have so many insisted that leadership equals an elitist club, not an embracing culture."

It is our opinion, substantiated by the surveys that an ego-based leadership style thwarts the essential development of future "*Uppercase leadership*." In other words, if a prime function of leadership is to ensure that the leadership pool is always being fueled, then why, by the very definition of leadership, eliminate so many?

Uppercase Leaders, Lowercase Leaders

The fire fighter on the tenth floor of an occupied apartment building may be called upon to lead – to influence. An available fire fighter may have to take initiative to influence the flow of traffic at a fire scene. A dispatcher may be presented with a scenario that is not covered by a policy or procedural manual. They will have to bring initiative and influence to task. Each of these persons will equal what we will refer to as *lowercase leaders.*

Chiefs, deputy chiefs, battalion commanders, and captains will be referred to as *Uppercase leaders*. There is significant distinction between the responsibility-factor and the influence-factor as related to *Uppercase leaders* and *lowercase leaders*.

Our surveys were completed by *Uppercase leaders*. Two separate themes emerged: 1) The responsibility to develop future leaders and 2) The responsibility to be held accountable as an *Uppercase leader*.

The Responsibility to Develop Future Uppercase Leadership

The first point of commonality between the respondents was a mandate to service the journey of *lowercase leaders*. This journey-servicing would hopefully help pave the way for a transition into *Uppercase Leadership*. What we learned from Fire-Rescue professionals did not surprise us. It was encouraging. Those who completed our surveys made very clear that they felt an internal mandate to help develop a leadership-pool.

****

"Your leadership pool is an ocean, not a pond."
-SMG

****

The Responsibility to be Held Accountable

The second theme that was established by our respondents was the relationship between responsibility and accountability. There was exhibited an acute awareness: "I am the one who must be held accountable."

This sentiment can be summarized in the following statement: "I cannot push a button and shift the responsibility. This is a load I must carry." It is reassuring that the Fire-Rescue leaders in our country indicate and illustrate a willingness to carry the burden and challenge of responsibility.

Influence as Inspiration, Not Imposition

Another strong thread that bound our respondents to each other related to inspiration. The power of the big "I," influence, has been referred to earlier. In this section, we must underscore that those who participated in our survey linked influence to inspiration, not to imposition. This is a radical leap from past models of leadership. The ability to lead is about influence, not about power. Influence is something you do. Power is something you have. The firefighter/rescue team member of today, except in emergency situations, does not respond favorably to power. Instead they follow someone because they want to, not because they have to.

History is packed with examples of leaders who exhibited influence, but it was a negative genre of influence. It was unusually authoritative. There was no dispensing of slack, no wiggle room, no hint of empowerment. It looked like this: "This is the way it must be – my way!"

One could argue that historical times mandated a different leadership focus and demeanor. That is not the focus of our book. We are seeking to paint a picture of lessons that are being learned today.

Before proceeding further, the perceived obvious must not be left for assumption. There is no doubt that there are occasions when *Uppercase leaders* must bring to task an influence that leads to imposition. A "caring enough to confront" is a mantra that must be held within the inner-life cupboard of ever authentic leader.

We feel sad when we realize that probably most people live their lives out of survival and resignation. They have fallen into that terrible pit of believing a lie. They feel that who they are does not make a difference – so they have given up, except for doing what it takes to just survive.

We can choose a lifestyle of making a difference. Making a difference is the core of influence. There are benefits to making a difference. One benefit is the enrichment we own by just having the right attitude. The second benefit is the feeling we have about ourselves. We will discuss difference will be addressed later in the book.

High on the Ladder

With the "caring enough to confront" and "necessary imposition" exceptions stated, influence as inspiration must be heralded. Influence at its best equals inspiration.

High on the survey-response ladder was the conviction that leadership is grounded in influence, slanted toward the positive, exhibited as inspiration. Our respondents saw their role as encouragers, not discouragers.

Not So Easy, Not So Fast

The journey toward influence as an inspiration and away from influence as an imposition has been laced with a challenge. This journey-path has not always been paved with ease and speed.

Lessons Learned...

One of the questions in our survey was: "What is the biggest mistake you have made as a leader?" Another question was: "What is the biggest weakness with which you struggle?"

The answers to these queries were similar in nature. They revealed a journey, in many cases, that was colored with struggle. They indicated a shifting in thinking – a shifting that was very personal in nature. The answers established that the move from imposition to inspiration was not always easy, nor fast.

For the most part, leaders responding to the survey stated that they would not make decisions the same way today that they did when they first started (If I had only known...). This indicates that leaders mature. The maturing of a leader is something the individual should recognize. Some things only come with time. You need the right foundation including: education, experience, intelligence, and patience.

"Failure is not an option." This quote was made famous by Tom Hanks who starred in the movie, *Apollo 13*. In reality, the statement was spoken by the famed NASA Flight Director, Gene Kranzen. This is an appropriate mantra for today's leaders to adopt.

****

"Leadership does not embrace quick fixes,
nor does it equal problems that can be
solved with a checkbook."
-JMB

****

Worth the Effort

Personal growth is never easy. Becoming an *Uppercase leader* is more complex than simple. The difficulty-level is high. It is complicated when imposition dominates and inspiration is stifled.

****

"None of us get to be right all of the time."
-JMB

****

The road toward "I have found it" (inspiration over imposition) is paved with zigs and zags. "Detourlessness" is an illusion. Traveling by detour is a reality for any authentic leader. Yes, a switch from "influence as imposition" to "influence as inspiration" is complex, often slow-moving in nature. But, the switching is worth the effort.

Who Benefits from the Switching?

We all do. *Uppercase leaders* and *lowercase leaders* have something in common. They both benefit when respecting influence as inspiration, not as mere imposition. The community served by this genre of leader profits from the switching.

A redefined leadership will underscore the fact that influence is the fulcrum of leadership. Where there is no influence, there is no leadership. But, factoring influence into your leadership equation is not the key task. The ultimate opportunity is to factor a positive influence (inspiration) into your leadership equation.

This is a complex challenge, neither easy, nor fast. But, it is worth the toil!

Leadership Is about the Person, Not the Position

When position is a prerequisite for leadership, the masses are eliminated. When leadership is defined by the position, and not by the person, that can equal form minus force.

If style is the extension of who you are coming through in everything you do (and it is), then your leadership style has more to do with you than the position you hold.

****

"A white shirt and gold bugles do not a leader make."
-Chief Stephen R. M. Moreno, III
Tarpon Springs, FL Fire Rescue

****

CHAPTER 2

Leading Yourself before You Lead Others

"Many view leadership as a science applied to others. The more I learn about leadership, the more I realize leadership is about self-reflection and challenging my own paradigms."
-Division Chief, Eddie Buchanan
Hanover Fire and EMS

"Tomorrow brings a new set of challenges, an opportunity to excel beyond today."
-JMB

"Leadership can equal the extension of your personality coming through in what you do, especially at the points of your influence. Authentic leadership will never ask you to be who you are not."
-SMG

****

"Be careful when opening the over-head bin as items tend to shift." The previous sentence is heard over our airwaves by airline attendants and their passengers thousands of times daily. It also sets the stage for this chapter in *Lessons Learned*.

Be cautious when you open your understanding of leadership. If you think leading the others is more important than leading yourself, then be careful, and think again. If you think leadership is all about "them," and never about "you," then your thinking must shift.

The participants in our study revealed an important shifting: "Leading yourself is essential if you are to lead others." Leaders cannot lead out from a vacuum. Where there is a void within, leadership remains only an illusion.

You Have What It Takes

Leadership is release, not implantation. You start with much more than nothing. There is already within each of us a leadership skills-set, perhaps raw and obscure, that can be claimed and polished. Let us emphasize again: "Leadership is not an elitist club. It is an embracing culture. It is not about position; it is about presence. Leadership is about influence. You have a tremendous capacity for influence."

****

"Deciding how to use the energy at your disposal is critical."
-JMB

****

We continue this segment with a story about Michelangelo. One day, he was pushing a huge rock down the street. From a chair on a porch, an elderly woman asked, "Michelangelo, why are you pushing that rock?" Michelangelo responded, "There is an angel inside that wants out."

Your first leadership act is to recognize the leader within you and "lead it out." You cannot lead the others if you refuse to lead yourself. Attempting to lead others while refusing to lead yourself is fraught with folly. You cannot give what you do not have. And, you will give what you do have.

Detecting a leadership angel within you is essential. But, it is not enough. Identifying the leadership potential within you is mandatory. But, it alone is not sufficient.

It is not enough to claim the leader within you. You must polish the leader within you. To polish is to practice. To polish is to lead – not merely think of leading.

You start with yourself. You lead from within.

How Do You Lead Yourself?

1) You honor who you are – a person of privilege.
2) You think of yourself not in terms of isolation, but in terms of inclusion.
3) You lead yourself by identifying your strengths and sculpturing those strengths.
4) You lead yourself to an Army of Allies and an Arsenal of Resources.
5) You celebrate incremental "Finished-ness."

****

"Quit watching the other guy; follow your gut instinct. You know the right thing to do."

- Raul A. Angulo, Captain,
Ladder Company 6
Seattle, WA Fire Department

****

Honor Yourself

Lead yourself to think about leadership in a fresh way.

If any one-word surfaced repeatedly in our study, that word was "privilege." To think of leadership from a different perspective is to honor leadership as a place of privilege. This concept riveted throughout the pages of our study.

Self-reflection often becomes more important to people in turbulent leadership times. Self-reflection is a critical component in honoring yourself and those whom you lead. Sometimes self-reflection can be a wake-up call to change. Change is not always bad.

In most cases, change can be for the good. If we constantly give of ourselves, if we do not take the time or make the effort to refill ourselves, we will not survive in today's world. We must first ask what we truly need before we can lead others.

Acceptance is the culmination of this pursuit for personal truth. We have been on a quest for self-discovery. What we have learned is that the answers to life's riddles cannot be found through the eyes of another, but rather through exploration within the self. Self-reflection can access your personal power to create happiness and fulfillment. This is not always easy. It can be uncomfortable. As Fire-Rescue leaders, we must live our lives as if we value and honor who we are.

****

"I don't think you have to be wearing stars on your shoulders or have 'commander' in your title to be a leader. Anybody who wants to raise his hand can be a leader any time."

-General Ronald R. Fogleman
US Air Force

****

Inclusion, Not Isolation

Leadership is broad enough to include you, important enough to include you, and honorable enough to include you. The needs and opportunities in today's world do not call for timidity, nor do they call for exclusivity. They mandate boldness; they call for you to claim the leader within you. Leadership is more than what (and who) is out there. Leadership is what is within there – within you.

There is a huge challenge here. It is related to how we think. We "think" ourselves down, not up; we "think" ourselves out, not in. Stop ruling yourself out. Invite yourself into leadership. Accept the invitation.

Sculpt Your Strengths

Lead from your strengths. Lead yourself beyond strength destruction or strength avoidance. Lead yourself toward strength development. Claim. Polish. Utilize. Then, polish more.

An Army and an Arsenal

Lead yourself toward an Army of Allies that will encourage you to build an agenda for personal growth. Lead yourself toward an Arsenal of Resources that will provide you with a reservoir of help-tools.

Celebrate Incremental "Finished-ness"

One challenge that we have observed in Fire-Rescue leaders across the country, is the temptation to become destination-driven to a fault. Survey after survey reflected the dominance of goals within the lives of our respondents.

For sure, goals provide leaders with initiative, focus, monitoring, and achievement. The problem with celebrating only at destination-arrival, is that it postpones celebration. Celebration is essential to growth.

The antidote for this malady is to lead the self into celebrating "incrementally." A celebration of first steps, then second steps, will contribute to, not diminish, leadership development. Lead yourself toward a driving gently with yourself. Lead yourself to celebrate along your growth-route.

Lead You

You will have opportunities to lead persons who will become noted as stellar leaders in their own right. You will be blessed with privileges to lead young children and senior citizens. Only He will know how many you lead.

An argument could be made that the most important person you lead is not the stellar future leader or the young children or the precious senior citizens. An argument could be made that the most important person you lead is "you." It starts the whole cycle.

****

"Before you can lead others, choose to lead yourself! Claim what is already within you, polishing, and polishing more.
-SMG

****

CHAPTER 3

Servicing Your Journey

"I service my journey by re-inventing my desire to serve my team members."

-Chief Stephen R. M. Moreno, III
Tarpon Springs, FL Fire Rescue.

"Demonstrate the imperative of accountability: making choices brings consequences – and bad choices bring bad consequences."

-JMB

"Service is a verb. It is not merely an act of kindness. It is what you do."

-SMG

****

The boomerang is an interesting device. Thrown properly, it returns to the center. When individuals service their journey, the journey servicing will equal a "re-energizing."

Our respondents blessed us with a plethora of "boomerang examples." These next paragraphs will catalogue various methods that leaders choose to utilize in servicing their journey.

Exercise

Chief Al Yancey of the Minooka, Illinois Fire Protection District referred to the power of exercise in his life not once, but twice, stating: "Regular exercise keeps me feeling good and keeps my mind sharp. I enjoy going to the gym, working out, and riding my bicycle."

Chief Mark Burdick of the Glendale, Arizona Fire Department words it differently: "I find my solace in tending to home chores and gardening."

Whether exercise takes place in the gym or in the garden, while riding a bicycle or raking leaves, it pays tremendous dividends in journey-servicing.

Volunteer

A change of perspective is healthy. A rattle in your car may seem significant, until you encounter someone who has no car. A small leak in your roof may seem highly problematic, until you encounter someone with no home. A very minor tension within your team can seem hugely problematic, until you encounter a team that is tearing itself apart.

Volunteering to help a team or an individual is therapeutic. It can change your perspective, remind you of how grateful you should be, and service you in body, mind, and spirit.

When you start feeling sorry for yourself as a leader, do not stay on the pot of pity. Do something. Service your journey. Volunteer!

Count

Flowing out from your volunteering will be the tendency to count your blessings. A concept that surfaced repeatedly in our study was the power of gratitude within the life of a leader.

The point that we would like to make is: do not merely count your blessings. Channel your blessings so they work for you, so they help you service your journey. Leverage and utilize your gratitude to work for you and for your leadership.

Gratitude need not be a back-end response. Gratitude can be a front-end "ignighter" and a rudder, servicing your journey beyond measure.

****

"He is a wise man who does not grieve for the things which he has not, but rejoices for those which he has."

-Epictetus

****

Family Time

"Time with my family is of prime importance." said Chief George Good of Tolleson, Arizona. He continued with a very critical point: "I dream about being with my family and children."

Chief Good speaks for legions of Fire-Rescue professionals who service their journey by not only being with their family, but by looking forward to being with their family. Anticipation of family time is a key way many leaders service their journey.

Laughter

Laugh. Although laughter is not always appropriate, a good laugh cannot only place things in perspective, but it also has proven physical benefits.

Both John and I are persistently laughing. We find it very beneficial, particularly in the midst of hectic travel schedules.

****

"A person without a sense of humor is like a wagon without springs. It's jolted by every pebble on the road."

-Henry Ward Beecher

****

Rest

Fatigue intensifies a drift toward "the dumps."

It was no surprise to us to learn that many Fire-Rescue respondents had difficulty with relaxation. For them, and perhaps for you, we suggest a delightful book. *When I Relax, I Feel Guilty* by Tim Hansel. This book was originally published in 1979. It will be difficult to find. At last resort, you may be able to talk to Stephen into loaning you his copy.

Start a New Project

Chief Fred Windisch shares how he services his journey: "I start a new project. Or, I talk to myself to assure that I am still focused as I attempt to eliminate negative feelings."

Pray

It would be inappropriate to conclude this section on journey-servicing and the re-energizing of oneself without sharing the following observation. Our respondent-leaders often referred to the one to whom Karl Barth referred to as the Holy Other.

The reference to prayer as a source for re-energizing was not casual. It was profound.

"Boomeranging"

The efforts you invest in re-energizing yourself and in servicing your journey will "boomerang" back to you in the dividends of a stronger leadership. What you do for yourself can enable you to do more for others.

****

"You cannot give what you do not have.

-SMG

****

CHAPTER 4

Loyalty Builds Followership

"You cannot be a good leader if you
do not know how to follow."
-Chief Forney Howard
Orange Beach, AL Fire & Rescue

"Loyalty remains one of the more critical components of leadership and followership."
-JMB

"It is appropriate to use terms such as 'leadership' and 'followership.' It is inappropriate to forget that there is a leader (either Uppercase or lowercase) within each of us. Those who lead, should follow. Those who follow can lead. There is a leader and a follower within you. Claim and polish each."
-SMG

****

Question number seven of our survey was among the most "open-ended" question we asked. We indicated that a book of this scope would cover many chapters. Then we asked, "What subject would you like to be covered in a particular chapter?"

Chief Rob Carnahan from the Tualitan Valley Fire and Rescue responded: "A chapter on followership is imperative somewhere near the beginning." Perhaps the most important word in the previous sentence is "beginning." It is loyalty that can birth followership. It is a void of loyalty that can fuel at best resentment, and at worst, rebellion.

Followership equals an enigma. It can flow out from both *Uppercase* and *lowercase leaders*. Loyalty can look like initiative, it can also resemble result. The axis upon which followership spins is loyalty.

Leaders produce followers; followers produce leaders! The glue that brings leaders and followers together, or the abrasive that can tear them apart is often an issue of loyalty. It is appropriate to use terms such as 'leadership' and 'followership.' It is inappropriate to forget that there is a leader (either *Uppercase* or *lowercase*) within each of us. Those who lead, should follow. Those who follow can lead. Loyalty will be the common denominator within the process. There is a leader and a follower within you. Claim and polish each.

Beware of the Loyalty Drought

Spring 2008 - deep has become shallow, plenty has been diminished by drought. The branches, streams, and creeks that poured into the river flow no more. Beds of stone have turned dry. This is not good.

Loyalty is a river fueled by three branches: Within Self, Out from Self, Into Self. Remove one of these branches and the loyalty-river begins to run dry as followership evaporates. Understand the inner-connectiveness of the three branches and followership can flourish. Appreciate loyalty as cycle and you take a critical step toward understanding the relationship between loyalty and followership.

****

"Trust is a learned behavior, as is distrust. It is a direct reflection of the team leader. If you do not have trust growing in your organization, start by looking in the mirror."

-JMB

****

Loyalty within Self

If trust is the cornerstone of loyalty (and it is), then trust never extends out from self unless it first resides in self. If you live in a world where you distrust yourself, where you sense no bonding within, a bonding that includes others will elude you.

The ebb and flow of loyalty only sputters unless loyalty begins within. Distrust programmed within breeds a distrust that is thrust out towards others. Instead of creating a sense of loyalty within your team, you project distrust, perhaps even paranoia.

Do not expect others to believe in you, to follow you, and to be loyal to you if they sense that you perpetually doubt yourself. How can you expect others to be loyal to you if you do not have the courage to be loyal to yourself.

Confidence Finds You

For several years, I have felt that confidence is not something you find. Confidence finds you when you are looking for something else, normally within a state of awkwardness. That something else is a growing sense of trust toward self, a sense of loyalty within. If you persistently program suspicion and distrust within yourself, confidence will refuse to find you.

This is a critical issue that must be explored further. If we refuse to have faith in ourselves, we will not be creating followership. If we refuse to be loyal to ourselves, we will be creating within ourselves attempts to confront or manipulate others. When confrontation and manipulation surface out from your refusal to be self-reliant, you discourage your team. You certainly do not inspire them.

Do not expect others to exhibit loyalty if they repeatedly perceive you as refusing to believe in yourself. This loyalty toward self, if taken seriously, is a discovery of a "comfort within."

Our studies indicate that the composite of trust, confidence, loyalty, and followership will never solidify, only crumble, where there is no integrity.

****

"Self-trust is the first secret of success...
the essence of heroism."
-Ralph Waldo Emerson

****

Integrity

A "comfort within," a sense of integrity, will remain illusive if you cannot agree with the following:

- I understand integrity as a "constancy within" - a cohesiveness between my sojourn (walk) and my speaking (talk). I am a person of integrity.
- I understand that purity of motive is an illusion. A persistent pursuit of purity of motive is my goal.
- I seek to "drive gently" with myself when I refuse to battle against myself, I remain inclined to stay "in like" with myself. This enables me to be both a better leader and a better follower. I understand with full force that "likability" is helpful for a Fire-Rescue leader. Others will not like me if I refuse to like myself.

****

"In order for people to put the 'we' in front of the 'me,' they need to feel confident that 'me' matters. They need to feel good about who they are and what they can offer. This requires a healthy degree of self-respect and self-esteem, a genuine belief that one adds value to the team."
-JMB

****

Lessons Learned...

- My "liking myself," can be taken too far resulting in arrogance, self-centeredness, egotistical.
- My "comfort within" is enhanced because I respect myself as an effective communicator. I appreciate the five elements of communication: source, message, channel, receiver, and perception. A more thorough discussion on communication will be in a later chapter.
- I can be loyal to myself because I am not lazy. I pay the preparation price.
- I am confident and competent - so much so that I do not have to "What-If?" myself all day long.
- I trust myself as a "choice person." I understand that choices create, confirm, and change circumstances. I trust myself at the point of discernment. This facilitates a loyalty within.

****

"I pray thee, O God, that I may be beautiful within."
-Socrates

****

- I think about the thoughts I think. I refuse to believe everything I think.
- I value myself as decisive - yet willing to dispense some slack. Whether as a follower or a leader, I have the courage to be the one for whom one can equal a lonely number. I trust myself to make the tough decisions.

- I can be loyal to someone like me because I care enough to confront.
- I trust myself because if I do not know what to do, I have the willingness to ask for help.
- I value myself because I fully understand that I must be the advocate for our Fire-Rescue department. This is my privilege.
- I can be loyal to someone like me because I do not take safety as anything less than a very serious business.
- I trust myself because I insist on reading at least one book a month. I hold the desire and capacity to learn.
- I am blessed with what I consider to be a strong sense of character and a proven set of skills.
- I am grateful that our team values me as a credible leader. This sense of gratitude (on the front-end) keeps me going.
- I would follow someone like me. If I could not, I would quit.

****

"Never ask people to do more than you are willing to do."
-JMB

****

- I understand that loyalty within, a followership extending out from the core of my persona is a critical first-link to the loyalty process. Without loyalty "within," there can be no loyalty "out from," and ultimately no loyalty "into self."

****

"Worry not that no one knows you;
seek to be worth knowing."
-Confucius

****

Loyalty Out from Self

You have been freed and equipped from the expression of loyalty that flows "out from you." You are empowered to give, not manipulate, or excessively confront. You have the capacity to present loyalty (from within) in such a fashion as to allow it to flow out from you toward others. The loyalty that takes wings as it flows from you to others becomes not only the glue that holds leadership and followership together. It also becomes a reinforcement that your creation of loyalty (from within) was valid and worthwhile.

****

"Are you modeling trust and integrity? Are you trustworthy? Are you covering for your team members? Are you honest with your department? Do you show up on time? The correct answers require a healthy degree of self-respect and self-esteem."
-JMB

****

Loyalty Is More Likely to Flow Out from You When:

In this section, we address simple steps, what we call loyalty-builders that will help you put meat on the bones of intention. We are seeking to answer these questions: "What can I do that expresses loyalty from me to another? What can I do that will exemplify a mutual followership? What does a loyalty that flows out from me, in very simple and realistic terms, look like?" Suggested answers to the preceding questions are:

- **Avoid the desk**. Imagine this scenario: You are in your office working behind your desk. A new officer enters the room and asks to speak with you. A smart, loyalty-building-move would be for you to leave your desk and sit right across from him or her, face to face. Territorially and spatially, you can eliminate loyalty barriers and minimize any tone of one "up-manship."

- **Do not collect stamps; use them.** It sounds so simple, yet it is so important. You can express loyalty toward another when you simply take time to write and mail a letter. Unfortunately, "e-mails" have become an example of strengths taken too far. Are you loyal enough to them to take the time to write personal notes?

- **Catch them doing well and translate.** Some choose to describe a breakdown of followership as that which results from our catching others doing poorly, but never catching them doing well. For most of us, this is not the case. It is not a matter of "catching" and "not catching." It is a matter of "catching and translating" when the issue is confrontation, and "catching" and "refusing to" translate when the issue is affirmation. Loyalty is not created when you catch them doing well and fail to translate. If you want to fuel followership, catch them doing well and translate. The "catching" is an attitude. The "translating" is a behavior.

- **Be a person of force.** Caution: This is not the same thing as "being forceful." To be a person of force simply means that you extend from yourself that which you are requesting from others. There must be a consistency between your expectation and your example. You do not simply want to be a person of "form." You want to be a person of force. The form minus the force equals a farce. To be a person of integrity is to be a person of force - not mere words. When asked, "What is your number one strength in fire and rescue?" Chief Michael VanZile of the Auburn, IN Fire Department hit the nail on the head with fourteen words: "I lead by example. All eyes are watching you when you are at the top." Chief Laurienti echoes Chief VanZile's sentiments when he writes: "A fundamental requirement for a Fire-Rescue leader is to lead by example."

****

"Expectation minus example equals exasperation."
-SMG

****

- **Think twice about assigning parking spaces.** Again, territorially and spatially, you can indicate an one "upmanship" when you set aside certain privileges for yourself. Loyalty is created when you think about things from their perspective.

- **Listen to yourself before you speak.** Imagine, ahead of time, the consequences of what you are about to say before you say anything. Think about this point every time you brush your teeth. Toothpaste comes out of the tube easily, but you cannot put toothpaste back into the tube. Our harsh words are often uttered in haste. We speak before we listen to what we are getting ready to say. We are faced with a problem. We cannot take our words back. What we have heard as a child is not true: "Sticks and stones can break your bones, but words cannot hurt you." This is not true.

- **Seek inspiration.** You are in a groove. You have recognized the opportunity to present a loyalty that has been "within" in such a fashion that it becomes a loyalty "out from you." You resolved that you would express loyalty. You respond by expressing loyalty. But, something happens. You start reneging, and regressing. Re-visit your opportunity for projecting loyalty "out from" yourself. Seek inspiration: network, read, walk, pray, get away from it all.

- **Listen to them.** If you, as a Fire-Rescue leader, want to invite your team members to take ownership of an inventory of new ideas, then be willing to listen to them. Chief Fred Windisch of the Ponderosa, TX Fire Department has it right: "I am absolutely committed to listening to new ideas that spawn creative thinking."

****

"We have two ears and one mouth so that we can listen twice as much as we speak."
-Epictetus

****

- **Balance!** Here "balance" is a verb. The issue of balancing surfaced many times in our surveys. As a matter of fact, Chief Michael VanZile of the Auburn, IN Fire Department referred to this issue as critical, particularly when one is a leader of a combination fire department (20 career, 25 volunteer). He suggested that this might be the toughest job there is, the job of balancing. Chief VanZile refers to this challenge as "the balancing act."

- **Re-visit balancing.** Loyalty can only build followership when one understands the relationship between strengths and weaknesses. Most any strength can be taken too far - so far as to become problematic: when eye contact equals a stare, when teasing equals torture, when friendliness diminishes objectivity. Loyalty can only build followership when you balance your strengths with your weaknesses. Pay particular attention to the following quote.

****

*"My number one strength within Fire and Rescue is my **open-mindedness**. My number one weakness in Fire and Rescue is **self-assertion**."*

-Chief Ross Elmore
Petersburg, VA Fire Dept.

****

If you want to marry loyalty to followership, then bring discernment, or "the balancing act" to task. Consistently, seek to monitor excesses. If your strength is talking, work on listening. If your strength is organization, be patient with those who are disorganized. If your strength is analysis, do not become bound to analysis. And, as in Chief Elmore's case, do not take open-mindedness so far as to diminish your capacity to assert yourself.

Loyalty into Self

If the cyclical nature of loyalty and followership is to run its course, then element number three, "Loyalty into Self" cannot be ignored. This is a delicate issue because it involves "receiving." As you well know, this is very difficult for many of us.

The loyalty/followership cycle is dynamic. It builds departments, ignites teams, inspires individuals. However, it can come to an abrupt halt if you are not careful.

My yard held on its turf, a huge pine tree for forty years. Do you know how long it took to cut down that tree? It took less than four minutes.

****

"Loyalty is a river fueled by three branches:
Within Self, Out from Self, Into Self."
-SMG

****

You can dedicate years of your life to creating a "loyalty within." You can, with both intensity and authenticity, project loyalty "out from yourself." If you stop there, you are not even coming close to reaching the maximum benefit of the loyalty/followership cycle. In fact, to say you are spinning your wheels may not be strong enough. A cycle that took years to begin will be destroyed the moment you refuse to receive loyalty/followership/inspiration from others.

We must understand that to refuse to accept back in to ourselves the gift of loyalty/followership is interpreted by our team members as a blatant rejection. This issue is as simple, and as complex, as our refusal to receive compliments as well.

Excessive verbiage at this point is unnecessary. Allow team members to service your journey.

****

"The capacity to receive can equal a grand gift."
-SMG

****

Note: Although each of these books listed here address issues beyond the scope of this chapter, their contribution to the subject of this chapter is so significant as to mandate a special listing:

- *The Speed of Trust* by Stephen M. R. Covey, 2008
- *The Likability Factor* by Tim Sanders, 2005
- *The Loyalty Effect* by Frederick F. Reichheld, 1996

CHAPTER 5

Creating Personal Excellence

"A person who has good character has everything. This is one of the qualities that institutions cannot bestow upon you. Compassion is as fundamental as honesty. We see people on their worst days. If we cannot be compassionate, we should not be in the business."

-Chief Luther Fincher
Charlotte, NC Fire Dept

"Tell your firefighters that perfection is seldom achieved, but that what you gain in the pursuit of excellence is most valuable."

-JMB

"'Sitting around' waiting for happy endings does not craft personal excellence. Personal excellence does not merely happen. It must be created. The root of the creation is choice."

-SMG

****

Lessons Learned is, by intent, designed to emphasize key concepts. The essential elements of this book will surface more than once. It is our intention to stress the content of what we have learned by addressing it from different perspectives in several chapters.

Six words will join many chapters to each other. These same words will equal the answer to the following question. "How do you create personal excellence?"

Above-the-cut leaders will pass the 9C test: Character, Competency, Confidence, Compassion, Commitment, Credibility, Courage, Concentration, and Classification (of priorities). These words are from the core of a quest toward personal excellence. We are acutely aware that there is a tenth C: Communication. Later, we will address communication as a key component of personal excellence, leadership and perception at length.

Character

Character is paramount. Personal excellence minus a strong character is nothing more than an illusion. Leaders void of character will eventually experience long nights.

Unfortunately, your character-mold is already partially set. But, it need not be set in concrete. Past performance does not have to be indicative of future results.

Surround yourself with persons of high character. The law association is not a myth; it is a reality.

Make wise choices. You can spend thirty years to build a solid character. You can destroy that your good character in less than thirty minutes.

Learn to imagine the consequences of bad choices before you make the choices. "What if-ing" in the positive sense can save you both embarrassment and costly consequences.

****

"Character is power."

-Booker T. Washington

****

Competency

Competency is the quiver that holds the arrows of a skills-set. The ability to do some things well is a leader's mantra.

Take the first steps that lead to extra knowledge. Pursue, with full vigor, the capacity to soar beyond success. Remember, practice does not make perfect. Practice will make for "better."

Competency is an enigma. Once you think you have reached the top, you have not. Once you think you know there is all to know, you do not. Once you think you have arrived, you are not there.

****

"Experience is important;
knowledge is critical."
-JMB

****

Competency, in relationship to personal excellence, is perpetually being redefined. The exciting news is this: You are in the driver's seat.

The test of competency is an "inner" test. To recall what Coach John Wooden said of his father will be very helpful:

My dad, Joshua, had great influence on my personal definition of success, and it has little to do with fortune or fame. Although, I probably didn't really understand it at the time, one of the things he tried to get across to me was that I should never try to be better than someone else. Then he always added, 'But Johnny, never cease trying to be the very best *you* can be. That is under your control. The other isn't.'

Confidence

What we have been taught about confidence is wrong. We have been encouraged to find confidence: "If you are to achieve personal excellence, you must find confidence. Confidence is important."

Those who say confidence is important are correct. Those who suggest that we can find confidence are incorrect. You do not find confidence; confidence finds you. Confidence will find you when you are looking for something else. Confidence is most likely to find you when you have paid the preparation price.

****

"Often, confidence has the capacity to show up at the very point when you feel most awkward."

-SMG

****

Compassion

We hesitate to mention this. We do not intend to dilute an emphasis on the importance of any of the other five C's. We have chosen to state it: Our study indicated, that of all the "C" words, compassion was among the top listed.

It is interesting to note that there was, at least, an implied linkage between the privilege of leadership and the call toward compassion. Chief Fincher of the Charlotte, North Carolina Fire Department was right on target when he stated, "We see people on their worst days. If we cannot be compassionate, we should not be in the business."

Compassion keeps you "others-centered" and off the pity pot. Personal excellence never rises within your pity pot.

****

"There are three traits that define a great leader. They are vision, compassion, and resolve. Compassion is at centerpoint for a reason."

-Chief Stephen R. M. Moreno, III
Tarpon Springs, FL Fire Rescue

****

Commitment

Commitment will keep you "task-centristic." The capacity to give up quickly will not travel with a quest toward personal excellence.

If you think commitment is waning, deal with it while it is a leak, before it becomes a downpour. Commitment demands attention. Void attention, commitment will fade. Determination will dwindle. Discipline will falter.

Personal excellence mandates that your commitment be more than fickle. Personal excellence demands a commitment that is firm.

Binding oneself to commitment is not the same thing as binding oneself to perfection. As a matter of fact, relieving yourself from an incessant quest toward perfection may accelerate your move toward personal excellence. Commitment is a process, not a single event.

It is a process that must always be guarded. A poor choice at a single event can significantly harm the commitment process.

Commitment mandates your best self, not your perfect self. It calls for the discipline, not destruction, of the person. Indeed, the quest toward personal excellence embraces the very extension of who you are.

****

"I had to make the commitment to be a true leader and to do what was right for the benefit of my staff, my organization, my mission, and most importantly, the customer."

-Chief David B. Fulmer
Miami, OH Township Fire/EMS

****

Credibility

Credibility equals believability. Believability requires integrity. One could argue that the only strength that cannot be taken too far is integrity.

Credibility, integrity, and consistency travel with each other. In relationship to the consistency/element, Chief David Fulmer from the Miami, Ohio Fire and EMS will write: "Consistency is so important in our business. The work which we do is so fluid that often times the only thing holding it together is our leadership."

Credibility will not occur void of respect. You do not go out and demand respect; you go out and lead with authenticity and respect finds you. The enemy of credibility is manipulation. The friends of credibility are knowledge, consistency, and vulnerability.

****

"What is powerful is when what you say is just the tip of the iceberg of what you know."

- *Jim Rohn*, CPAE
International Speaker

****

Courage

In *Lessons Learned*, you will repeatedly encounter the 6R's of personal growth: Recognition, Resolve, Response, Reneging, Regression, and Re-visitation. For point of emphasis, and although it touches on each element, courage falls underneath "resolve."

Courage transcends commitment. Courage equals that extra grace that may call for commitment when difficulty, not ease, is the path you must follow.

Courage equals that visit to the inner-life cupboard, that time spent in the crucible of internal mandates. Courage rises out from awkwardness, ambivalence, and significant anxiety. Courage is often a tough, but necessary, call.

****

"Courage is not simply one of the virtues, but the form of every virtue at the testing point."
-C. S. Lewis

****

Concentration

Concentration helps you avoid focus-folly; determination-dwindling, and thought-tyranny. Concentration collapse will occur. Face it. Full concentration at every point, all the time, is an illusion. Concentration retrieval is not an illusion. Expect to lose a high level of concentration. Expect to recapture a high level of concentration.

Concentration is elusive. Keep your eye, heart, and mind on your task.

****

"Concentration is the secret of strength."
-Ralph Waldo Emerson

****

Classification (Prioritization)

****

"Make sure that safety is your highest priority."
-JMB

****

A listing of *Lessons Learned from Fire and Rescue Leaders* is blemished if it does not address the issue of classification. The bulk of this session is on the subject of the relationship between personal excellence and establishing priorities. You may ask: "Then why begin the section on the subject of classification?"

That is a relevant question. We have a simple answer. You will not be able to prioritize effectively if you do not first classify. Prioritization without classification handicaps your effort at establishing priorities before you start. If you want to prioritize, then first classify.

Classification is the starting point, the foundation, the critical first step toward establishing priorities. Not only is classification a simplification process, it is a structural procedure, grounded in priorities.

****

"Make these your priorities: Create common grounds, loosen dead locks, create specific expectations and qualifications."
-JMB

****

The Three Barrels of Classification

Classification addresses the concept of "sorting." Naturally before you sort, you must have something to sort. You create an agenda of items that you think must be addressed. This listing (broad in scope) need not carry with it a tremendous load of immediate and heavy consideration – at least not at this time.

Before you begin to face a broad grouping of issues, your smartest "first-step" is to classify those issues into one of three barrels: Do, Drop, or Delegate. You stack your "prioritizing" odds in your favor. You analyze your issue-list and classify: "This I must do. This I must drop. This I must delegate."

The significance of the relationship between priorities and personal excellence is a fundamental issue of concern for Fire and Rescue leaders. Repeatedly, the Fire and Rescue leaders we studied reflected struggle at this point. There was a minor reluctance to dropping an issue; there was major resistance, in many cases, in the area of delegation.

The truth that must not be ignored at this point is "Am I sifting? Am I holding on to what I must do? Am I releasing what should be dropped? Am I delegating where delegation is appropriate?"

You help yourself when you think of prioritization in relationship to the opportunity of classification. It is as simple, and it is as difficult as: Do, Drop, or Delegate.

Priority number one for you must be the issue of classification. It will help you service your journey, and ultimately the journey of your team.

Do

There are some items on your large composite of issues that must remain on your list. These items are your responsibility. A shifting into the wastepaper basket or a delegation alternative is inappropriate. These are your issues to hold – and to address.

Drop

You whittle your list once you choose to drop, permanently or temporarily, certain items from that list. In effect, you say to yourself: "This need not be done; or, this need not remain on this particular priority list – perhaps placed into a bin of 'for later consideration.'"

Delegate

You chisel your list further when you distribute responsibilities to a member of your command staff or in another direction. Under the umbrella of "control and uncertainty," you find the courage to delegate. The issue of delegation will be addressed later in this book and in our Recommended Reading list.

Now You Are Ready

You have narrowed your list of to-do items. Now you are prepared to order or rank your list. "Ordering" is not a haphazard structuring of responsibility. It mandates "method." Method requires "structure." Prioritizing is a systematic arrangement of pursuit grounded in order of significance.

Personal excellence is enhanced once you discover (or re-discover) that "choosing how to prioritize is remarkably important." Fire and Rescue leaders will often say something similar to this: "Prioritizing need not be as difficult as I have previously thought. For me, the answer lies within a process that simplifies things for me."

Simplification and the Top Nine

1) **Define the term**. We have chosen to define this term in a language that seems to be most appropriate. Therefore, let us think of prioritizing as "laddering" according to significance. Let us begin by asking the following questions: "Before I address rung number two, I must first focus on rung number one." Laddering is rooted in "what-ifing." "Addressing the first rung before I climb to the next rung, will I be serving the team and myself appropriately?" The pursuit of personal excellence mandates "questioneering:" "Have I ranked, laddered, or prioritized in an appropriate order? Have I ordered my agenda based on what requires my 'close at hand' attention?"

2) **Think in terms of alignment**. As you begin to prioritize, ask this question: "Will my short term prioritizing enhance or dwarf my long term needs? Is there alignment between mission and values (attitudes) and the laddering and the pursuit of future activity (behavior)?"

3) **List**. Begin with a random listing of "things to do." This listing consists of "the remainder from your do, drop, delegate technique. At this time, order is irrelevant. This is not the place for wasting time. Excessive reflection can be postponed. Remember that this is your "to-do" list. "Classification" has already narrowed the list through the do, drop, delegate technique.

4) **Avoid thought evaporation**. The place for this list is not in your head; it is "on paper." Protect your list. Remember: "What you think you will never forget can equal what you will forget." There is a "prioritizing" value in writing it down.

5) **Sort further**. You have already classified a larger list into your "to-do" list. At this point, you will no longer think about three barrels. You dwell on five baskets. It is our experience that "five" is a workable number. At least for purposes of this book, that number will prove both appropriate and helpful.

6) **Number your baskets 1-5.** Place your most significant "to-do" item in basket one. The least significant item falls into basket five. The speaker and author, Stephen Covey addresses the issue of significance in a stellar fashion.

7) **Rely on three questions**. As you place your issues into one of five baskets ranked according to significance, you will be assisted by a process that equals three questions. These questions are: "What? Why? How?"

8) **What?** Describe the issue. What does this issue address? What does it look like? What is its impact short term and long term?

9) **Why?** Analyze the issue. Why should this situation be pursued? Why does it merit a place on the list? If you struggle at the point of "why?" then you may need to re-examine, or remove, that particular "what?" The "why?" question will definitely help you rank or ladder your priorities.

****

"If you don't have a good Why? then you better find a different What?"
-SMG

****

10) **How?** If item number eight equals description, item number nine equals diagnosis, then item number ten equals prescription. How are you going to respond? How will you deal with this? The degree of clarity with which you are able to answer your "how?" questions will further assist you in prioritizing. If you have difficulty pursuing the entire "What? Why? How?" prioritizing process, then that priority will require further examination.

11) **Get a second opinion**. Often, after you have taken steps 1-10, the first thing you may pursue is another perspective. We are finding that Fire and Rescue leaders are increasingly asking their command staff a question similar to this: "Where do you think my efforts can

best be focused? This is my definition of my role here, do you see things differently?" For example, when Stephen and John are asked to speak for fire service associations and departments, they receive a particular request: "Would you please address role clarification?"

12) **Learn**. Prioritizing is rarely a single event. It is a process. It is another area where you can learn from your "where you have been." Past performance need not be indicative of future results.

13) **Read**. We have often stated that the first letters of Ready are R-E-A-D. The arsenal of resources that includes books is remarkable. There are a plethora of books listed near the end of this work that address both the quests for personal excellence and the role prioritizing plays in that journey.

At this point, we have recommended two books that might be of further help: *Juggling Elephants – An Easier Way to Get Your Most Important Things Done – Now!* by Jones Loflin and Todd Musig and *Developing the Leader within You* by John C. Maxwell. Pay particular attention to Chapter two, beginning on page 19, "The Key to Leadership: Priorities."

****

"The tools that can calm our nerves and open our minds are: courage, optimism, humility, humor, intuition, acceptance, forgiveness, love, and yes, patience."

-JMB

****

Your Leadership Style

Personal excellence in relationship to leadership will never ask you to be who you are not. You are unique and wondrously made. Your capacity to soar beyond mere success, to approach significance, is enhanced once you seek to recognize the 9C challenge: Character, Competency, Confidence, Compassion, Commitment, Credibility, Courage, Concentration, and Classification. Communication will be addressed in Chapter 14.

If you bring to task a positive Direction of thinking, a firm Discipline of approach, and a genuine Delight in journey, you stack the creation of personal excellence in your favor. It is an essential 1-2-3 punch: Direction, discipline, and delight.

****

"Do not discipline when angry."
-JMB

****

In the five word phrase "The quest for personal excellence," the most important word is "personal." Authenticity can never be trumped. Any excellence grounded in the superficial must be re-examined periodically. Form minus force will equal farce. You cannot be grounded in personal excellence and stray from "the real you" at the same time.

Drive gently with yourself. Ponder the direction of your thinking. Think about the thoughts you think and refuse to believe everything you think. Visit the discipline of your approach. Refuse the temptation to give up too quickly. Guard against "quitting before you quit." Finally, bring toward your quest for personal excellence an approach that is grounded in delight.

Personal excellence will mandate the ordering of choice over chore and opportunity over mere obligation. In one sense, it is as if you do not find personal excellence. Personal excellence finds you, often within a culture of awkwardness when you choose to pay the preparation price – and when you choose to be you.

****

"We are that which we repeatedly do.
Excellence, therefore, is not an act but a habit."
-Aristotle

****

CHAPTER 6

An Army of Allies, An Arsenal of Resources

"I rely greatly on a very short list of mentors, one being a formal fire chief, one being a pastor, and one being just a good long time friend. I get inspiration from leadership books."
-Chief Al Yancey
Minooka, IL Fire Protection

"Leadership is a skill that requires caring and supportive relationships within and outside the fire service."
-JMB

"When your world wobbles, when stumbling, not soaring, seems to be your mantra, when your leadership feels shaky, find help."
-SMG

****

Leadership is lonely. However, you do not have to do it alone! You can build an Army of Allies and an Arsenal of Resources.

"Build" is a verb. It is an action verb. There is nothing passive about the verb "build" or the gerund "building." Building is not an attitude, but it requires a positive attitude. Building is not only a desire, a hope, or mere strategy. Building is a behavior.

There Is No Substitute for Your Accountability

The preceding emphasis on building stresses there is something *you* must do. It travels along with a concept that you are responsible for leading yourself, for creating personal excellence, for leading others, and for servicing the journey of your team.

Implicit in this section is the concept that there is no shift-the-blame button. Accountability for who you are and for what you do lies at your feet.

Ultimately, sitting around and waiting for happy endings or waiting for a motivator will not serve you well. You must take responsibility for your actions.

****

"A bad habit never disappears miraculously.
It is an 'undo-it-yourself' project."
-JMB

****

An Army of Allies

There is help within you. You have experienced awkward situations before. You survived those situations and you will again.

Your help lies within you. The peace and presence that you cannot figure out, that comes from within, is Him.

There is also help that extends beyond you. This assistance falls into two categories: An Army of Allies and an Arsenal of Resources.

The respondents to our surveys agreed with each other at the point of reliance upon their Army and their Arsenal. Where they disagreed was at the point of the particulars.

Most Fire-Rescue leaders listed other fire chiefs at the top of their Army of Allies list. Others listed area leaders outside Fire-Rescue. Some shared the importance of team members, their spouses, their associates from the National Fire Academy, their pastor, or a friend.

Caution: Atrophy Ahead

Later in *Lessons Learned*, we will address the leadership challenge behind taking strength too far. If reliance upon an Army of Allies and/or an Arsenal of Resources is taken too far, the leadership within you will diminish.

The shriveling of your potential will be a likely consequence of your taking the reliance on others so far that it becomes problematic. Equilibrium is the goal. Balance is the key. Discernment is essential.

An Arsenal of Resources

Your Army of Allies is a personal pool of help. Your Arsenal of Resources is not as personal in nature. The fact that it is impersonal does not limit its impact or affect the wealth of information available to you.

With amazing clarity, our participants supported each other in lifting up the influence of books on leadership. This was such a significant portion in the Arsenal of Resources input that we will conclude this chapter with a section on books as vital resources.

Other than books, our respondents included the following in their Arsenal of Leadership Resources: International Association of Fire Chiefs, National Fire Academy, Local Fire departments, and web searches.

Ready begins with R-E-A-D

Most of us are familiar with The Rain Forest – that vast swath of land that is so important to our environment, indeed to our world. In similar fashion, there is The Gain Forest – a broad Arsenal of Resources essential to our leadership development.

The core of this Arsenal equals the books you read. Reading is the front door into The Gain Forest. You enter with The Given (what you already know); you secure The Gathered (what you read); The Given plus The Gathered equals The Growth.

Influence and inspiration of ten take residence on the written page. The books you read allow you to benefit from that influence and inspiration. The magic happens when what you choose to absorb becomes what you live and what you share.

Books allow you to benefit from the thinking and the perspective of people who live decades ago. Books extend the impact of the individual author far beyond their life span.

Some Specifics

We asked our respondents to list specific books that have been helpful to them in their leadership-journey. Instead of printing a Books on the Subject List at book's end, we chose to list "specific" books as shared by a limited number of our respondents (and by JMB and SMG).

1) The single most important leadership script for me has been a short little book entitled: *The Leadership Secrets of Santa Claus.* I use it frequently to review my behavior with regard to my co-workers. The book is published by The Walk The Talk® Company, Dallas, Texas. Other books helpful to me are: *Winning 'Em Over* by Jay A. Conger and *What Do They See When They See You Coming?* by Stephen M. Gower.

Chief Stephen R. M. Moreno, III
Tarpon Springs, FL Fire Rescue

2) I find that sometimes my greatest inspirations come from authors on subjects outside the fire service. I think the last leadership book I read, cover-to-cover, if it can be considered a leadership book was *Man's Search for Meaning* by Viktor Frankl. I have read a number of books on leadership over the years and would be hard-pressed to recommend only three. I would probably list some basic, often cited ones like: *Seven Habits of Highly Effective People* by Stephen Covey, *Credibility: How Leaders Gain and Lose It, Why People Demand It* by Barry Z. Posner and James S. Kouzes, and *The Fifth Discipline: The Art and Practice of the Learning Organization* by Peter M. Senge.

Chief Mark S. Burdick, M.A., CFO
Glendale, AZ Fire Department

3) The book I would recommend to other leaders is: *When In Doubt, Lead!: The Leader's Guide to Enhanced Employee Relations in the Fire Service* by Dennis Compton. It is a three-part series that, in my opinion, has changed how I lead.

Chief Michael Van Dyke
Montezuma Rimrock, AZ Fire District

4) I am hard pressed to move beyond Jim Rohn, America's Foremost Business Philosopher, when listing a writing style and a content that have been helpful to me. The simplest way to get a feel for this tremendous resource is to read: *The Treasury of Quotes* by Jim Rohn. Close behind, I will suggest: *You Don't Need a Title to be a Leader* by Mark Sanborn, *The Velveteen Rabbit* by Margery Williams, *The Precious Present* by Spencer Johnson, and any of the several books by Coach John Wooden.

-SMG

Speaking of Speakers

Under the Arsenal of Resources category, we must include the speakers to whom our respondents referred. This list is not all inclusive but it does point to the direction in which our participants were thinking.

We recognize there are many gifted speakers who are not on this list. Our intention is to focus on them in another publication. The speakers to which our respondents referred as being of particular benefit will be listed in alphabetical order:

Terry Bradshaw, Alan Brunacini, Bill Bryson, John M. Buckman, III, Carnagie speakers, Dennis Compton, Stephen Covey, Rudy Giuliani, Stephen M. Gower, Gordon Graham, Dr. Dale Henry, Tom Peters, and Edward O. Wilson.

The Ticking Clock

As we work on this particular chapter, we are both in a reflective state. There is no talking, no sound emanating out from the computer; all we can hear is the ticking of the clock.

For each of us, the clock ticks. Time at its slowest is fleeting. Our challenge is to maximize every moment, to harness every hour. We must not only examine how we manage time; we must also examine the energy we release moment after moment.

A wise use of time and energy equals three steps: 1) The acquisition of accountability, 2) The support of an Army of Allies, 3) The benefit of an Arsenal of Resources.

****

> For support and ideas, I turned to an Army of Allies. This equals my core of officers. Depending on the issue, decision-making processes may include only chief officers. Other situations will include engine company officers. I also learned much from great fire service leaders with whom I have had contact.
> For my Arsenal of Resources, I read a lot of Ron Coleman's work as well as Goldfeder's works on safety. The speakers and authors who mean so much to me are Howard Cross, NFA Instructor, Don Manno, Fire Service GURU, and Stephen M. Gower.

-Chief Stephen R. M. Moreno, III
Tarpon Springs, FL Fire Rescue

****

CHAPTER 7

Sculpting Your Strengths

"One of my strengths is that I remind myself that we are all charged to do the best job we can, everyday. I often say, 'The hardest thing any of us face is getting up in the morning with the attitude I will do my absolute best, even when I am not feeling my best.'"

-Chief Mark Burdick
Glendale, Arizona Fire Dept.

"Focusing on your firefighter's strengths instead of their faults will build their self-confidence and make them look at other people's strengths."

-JMB

"Strength sculpting is a 1-2 punch: Attitude and behavior. What is asleep within you will bless you – if you choose to awaken it."

-SMG

****

Many of us grew up being taught that K-I-S-S meant "Keep It Simple Stupid." This book is a strong re-buff against that opinion. People do not grow when you remind them of how stupid they are; that is when they self-destruct. People grow when you remind them how smart they are; that is when they self-correct.

To claim and polish the leader within you is to discover (and rediscover) the strengths within you – and then sculpt those strengths. Contrary to the opinion of some, personal growth is more likely to occur as a result of strength sculpting than as a result of weakness chiseling.

Strengths undiscovered and strengths undeveloped equal strengths wasted. On Sundays, many of us focus on stewardship. We should also be challenged to focus on stewardship during the work-phase of our lives.

We have been blessed with the capacity to do some things well. Routinely, there is a strong relationship between what we do well and what we love to do.

Lessons Learned is a clarion call to say, "yes" to your strengths, to isolate those strengths, to utilize them, and to persistently seek to improve them.

About "Centering on Self"

There is a huge gap between appropriate "centering on self" and self-absorption. The core of this chapter is actually an invitation. It is an invitation to visit, not a building or an event, but yourself.

St. Augustine exhibited a stellar capacity to articulate the difficulty we have with celebrating ourselves: "Men go forth to wonder at the heights of mountains, the huge waves of the sea, the vast compass of the ocean, the courses of the stars; and they pass by themselves without wondering."

As you center on yourself, it is our hope that you will encounter a skills-set that is uniquely yours. Our hope, indeed our belief, is that you will soar beyond success as a leader precisely while you are sculpting your strengths.

Poor Stewardship Equals a Personal Strength Wasted

By now, you have recognized where you are gifted: Perception, Organization, Discernment, Encouragement, Technical (computer), Mathematics, Patience, Caring enough to confront, etc. With this very section, we are encouraging you with a full-force vigor to lead with your strengths. Say, "yes" to who you are and where you have been blessed. Say, "yes" by recognizing, utilizing, and sculpting.

Strengths As Shared By Our Respondents

Fire-Rescue leaders equal "diversity within a unity." As a group, respondents were gracious in sharing their strengths. The strengths they shared, however, were not always the same. This of course was to be expected.

We thought it would be helpful if we shared with you what some of the respondents had to say in relationship to strengths. Our specific question was: "What is the number one strength you have as a leader in Fire-Rescue?" Some of their answers follow.

Lessons Learned...

1) When I was active, my *reputation* was one of being able to work with anyone. Today, I am an emergency manager and that reputation still stands.

Ken Knipper
Kentucky NVFC Director

2) My number one strength is an *open mind*.

Chief Ross Elmore
Petersburg, VA Fire Dept.

3) My greatest strength is in *identifying future leaders* and *growing others* to be great leaders. I have always tried to coach or guide others into more responsible positions.

Rob Carnahan
Tualitan Valley, OR Fire and Rescue

4) I lead by *example*. All eyes are watching you when you are at the top.

Chief Michael VanZile
Auburn, IN Fire Department

5) My greatest strength is the *high standard* I hold myself.

Robert Rielage
Moscow, OH Fire Department

6) People *trust* me to do the right thing at the right time.

Chief Harry Carter, Ph.D. (Retired)
Adelphia, N.J. Fire Company

7) I am *available*, willing to lift the heavy load, and not afraid of risk taking in the decision-making-process.

Chief Fred Windisch
Ponderosa, TX Fire Department

8) My greatest strength is *technical experience* and the ability to apply *knowledge* on the emergency scene.

Chief Ulysses Seal
Bloomington, MN Fire Department

9) Showing *enthusiasm* is my greatest strength; I believe in helping/giving back. I love what I do. This is truly a gift that we have the opportunity to serve.

Chief Jim Grady, III
Frankfort, IL Fire District

10) My greatest strength is *dedication* (commitment).

Ty Dickerson

Character and Competency

If you will recall, there were 9C's in our section on Personal Excellence. It is important to note that two of those C-elements were Character and Competency. Each of our previously listed strengths fall into one of those two barrels. It is our belief that the strengths you celebrate also fall into these barrels as well.

3-D Glasses

For the second time in *Lessons Learned*, we refer to a model that will place meat on bones. If strength sculpting is to move beyond theory, then you need a structure. Our suggestion is a simple three-legged structure: Direction, Discipline, and Delight.

Direction

Think about the thoughts you think. Do not believe everything you think. Refuse to think so "lowly" of yourself. If you beat yourself down with the thoughts you think, you will inevitably beat down those you lead. If you seek to sculpt your strengths, beginning with a positive can-do attitude, you will encourage those you lead. Bring to your leadership task a positive direction of thinking. Do not imagine your leadership dreams not happening. Instead, imagine your leadership dreams happening successfully. Help your dreams happen by remaining positive about the strengths you have. Envision how those strengths will help you obtain your goals.

Discipline

Strength sculpting is never the result of a fickle approach. Strength sculpting will never rise out from timidity, half-heartedness, and hope minus strategy.

If your strength is speaking in public, it will never get better unless you work to make it better. Here, strength sculpting will equal paying the preparation price, hour-after-hour, day-after-day.

If your strength is bringing harmony out from discord, you will never improve unless you labor more diligently. Here, strength sculpting will equal learning everything you can about negotiating and working with difficult people.

If your strength is leading a team that has been broken at the point of morale, you will never soar beyond success unless you invest time and inertia. Here, strength sculpting will equal the refinement of patience and the expiation of initiative.

Delight

The two of us (JMB and SMG) share a joy in speaking and writing. Our delight in task accompanies us as we travel from place to place.

Your work will not be without detour. The detours will have less of a sting when you manage to delight in your work. Again, there is a remarkable marriage between strengths perpetually being sculpted and having joy and meaning at work.

A Privilege

Our participants echoed time and again: "The leadership opportunity I hold is a privilege." The degree to which one is committed at strength sculpting reflects the degree to which he approaches leadership as privilege.

****

"To do your best you have to increase the quality of your practice time, not the quantity. Practicing one's strengths is time spent well!"
-JMB

****

CHAPTER 8

Chiseling Your Weaknesses

"One weakness I have to chisel is: I learn fast and I assume that everyone around me learns at the same rate. Then I find myself looking down at them because they cannot keep up with me."
-Chief Ross Elmore
Petersburg, VA Fire Dept.

"Tell your firefighters that if they never made a mistake, it would mean they never did anything. Teach them if they must doubt, doubt their doubts and not their beliefs."
-JMB

"Remember, you do not have to stay the way you are.
You can leave your postponement-pouch.
Be sure you are not standing in your own way."
-SMG

****

For many years, I have addressed the issue of personal growth in my presentations. In this chapter, I am addressing one of the three elements of personal growth. As stated earlier, the other two elements of personal growth are: 1) Strength Sculpting and 2) Where you take one of your strengths and apply it to one of your weaknesses.

Let us restate, with a full force, that strength sculpting is the way most of us grow most of the time. It is also certainly true that there is personal growth when we isolate one of our strengths and apply it to one of our weaknesses.

Lessons Learned...

When weakness chiseling is the issue, I know from experience that there are three issues that surface the most in my presentations/interactions. At least 80% of the time the dominant weaknesses represented will be: impatience, procrastination, and public speaking. The lesson that I continue to learn is that impatience, procrastination, and a confidence about public speaking impede effective leadership. It will take persistence to address the issue of battling against a weakness. You will probably fall short many times before you succeed.

When addressing the issue of battling your challenges and becoming impatient in your progress, there is a marvelous example of inspiration. When you become inclined to forget that growth is rarely a single event; when you forget it is process-centered; when you stumble along your way, remember this story of one of our country's presidents.

If you feel as if the weakness you face is winning, if you feel as if you always fail, bring persistence to task. If you need inspiration, remember the journey of President Abraham Lincoln:

- Failed in Business 1831
- Defeated for Legislature 1832
- Failed in Business, again 1833
- Elected to Legislature 1834
- Sweetheart Died 1835
- Had Nervous Breakdown 1836
- Defeated for Speaker 1838
- Defeated for Elector 1840
- Defeated for Congressional Nomination 1843
- Elected to Congress 1846

- Defeated for Congress 1848
- Defeated for Senate 1855
- Defeated for Vice President 1856
- Defeated for Senate 1859
- Elected President of the United States 1860

****

"Persistence is the twin sister of excellence. One is a matter of quality; the other, a matter of time."
-Marabel Morgan

****

In our survey, the challenge of impatience surfaced many more times than did battles against procrastination or speaking in public. Perhaps you can identify with some of these impatience-related comments listed. In this instance, we will not list the names of individuals beside the very personal responses. Nevertheless, the responses will be helpful:

1) My greatest weakness is that I am too quick to react.

2) I need to work on listening better.

3) My level of expectations for myself and others is too high.

4) I hold others to the same high standard that I hold myself.

5) My greatest weakness is impatience. Some things just do not happen quickly enough for me.

6) I always felt my main weakness was impatience. When I saw something that had to be done, I found it difficult to understand delays.

The Model for Chiseling Weaknesses

"What do you have?" is the model we suggest for crafting an Agenda for Growth at the point of weakness chiseling. It unfolds in this fashion:

- What do you have?
  (What is the weakness you are addressing?)
- What do you want in its place?
  (What are you wishing for? What is your specific targeted outcome?)
- Why do you not have what you want?
- What do you need to do to get what you want?

It will be helpful to illustrate, briefly, how this model can work. We will example weakness chiseling in three areas: Impatience, Procrastination, and Speaking in Public.

Impatience

- What do you have?
  Impatience.
- What do you want in its place?
  Patience.
- Why do you not have what you want?
  Lack of self control, lack of respect for others, a disregard for how I am perceived, fatigue.
- What do you need to do to get what you want?
  Practice self control, learn to value others, value the power of perception, and get more rest.

Note: Whatever you feel you need to do, you need to break it down into small steps. Example: In order to practice self control I will take an anger management course, practice meditation, exercise, etc.

Procrastination

- What do you have?
  Procrastination.
- What do you want in its place?
  Decisive and definite action/response.
- Why do you not have what you want?
  No precise method of response, distraction, fear of error, lazy.
- What do you need to do to get what you want?
  Do, drop, or delegate. First, eliminate distractions; always try to do your best by paying the preparation price. Learn to delegate throughout the staff. Stop "sitting around and waiting for happy endings."

Speaking in Public

- What do you have?
  A lack of confidence concerning public speaking.
- What do you want in its place?
  Confidence.
- Why do you not have what you want?
  A misunderstanding of confidence; a misunderstanding of nervous energy; a fear of what others will think; a reluctance to pay the preparation price.
- What do you need to do to get what you want?
  Understand that confidence will find me, often in a state of initial awkwardness when I am looking for something else. I will not find confidence, it will find me. Understand that nervous energy can be my friend and work for me rather than against me; recognize that others are not even thinking about me; pay the preparation price (this ties in with a new understanding of confidence and nervous energy).

Some Final Observations

The before mentioned model is very sketchy. The idea is to continue to ask questions, and to be insistent upon specificity at the point of answers.

Celebration must be incremental. Example: Do not celebrate perpetual patience (an illusion). Celebrate one moment when you are more patient than you would have been in the past.

The model is flexible. Personalize it!

Although you are responsible for your weakness-chiseling, there are two previously mentioned arenas of support that you can visit. Utilize you Army of Allies (colleagues, counselors, mentors, family). Benefit from your Arsenal of Resources (books, trade journals, magazines, etc.).

There Is Power in Vulnerability

Caution must be exhibited in the area of vulnerability. Many will attest that sharing weaknesses with team members can be helpful, not hurtful. his is a strength that can be taken too far. dmission to your weaknesses may open more leadership doors than it closes.

Re-statement: The Key Lies within Persistence

Imagine a ring similar to a boxing, wrestling, or ultimate fighting ring. Visualize two fighters battling in that ring. One fighter is respected across the globe for his persistence. He is not big nor extremely muscular in stature; but he will not give up. Now look at the other fighter. His body is sculpted in a fashion that is intimidating. But, he has a weak chin and holds a reputation for giving up easily.

These fighters have names. Fighter number one is called "Persistence." Fighter number two is named "Give Up Easily." Time after time, "Persistence" will out-do and out-last "Give Up Easily." In fact, "Give Up Easily" will often throw in the towel, and on occasion "quit before he quits."

****

"Our strength grows out of our weaknesses."
-Ralph Waldo Emerson

****

CHAPTER 9

Think about the Thoughts You Think

"Most of the thoughts I think are grounded in solving problems and making plans."
-Chief Tommy Ayers
Toccoa, GA Fire Department

"Teach your firefighters the importance of self-talk. The advice they give to themselves is important, so they should make it positive."
-JMB

"What you say to yourself may be the most important words you speak."
-SMG

****

I enjoy telling the following story.

It was one hour of torture – needless torture on my part. I was speaking for a group of leaders in Las Cruces, New Mexico. The presentation of the morning had just ended. There would be lunch before the afternoon presentation. Prior to lunch, I was approached by a young man who said: "Do not leave before I have a chance to speak with you. I have some very important advice for you but will have to speak to you later." "Later" seemed to last forever. I do not remember what was for lunch. I do remember that I did not enjoy it – because I was worrying about the important advice.

"What if I had offended the city manager or department head? What if I had appeared to be ill prepared and 'robotical?' What if this particular group felt that I was totally irrelevant?" In fact, I had a bad case of the What-ifs!

Mercifully, the young man and I were able to have a brief conversation before my afternoon session: "Mr. Gower, you said in your presentation that you no longer ran because you do not have the time. You must take the time. Your body is a temple. You have already had one heart attack, take good care of yourself. Exercise!" I breathed a sigh of relief. What I had anticipated as callus confrontation was a compassionate concern. I had not only thought the worse, I had believed the worse. My imagination had run amuck. Thankfully, once again I was wrong.

The Sentiments of Our Respondents

We asked participants the following question: "How does your 'self-talk' inform your leadership?" We were encouraged by the responses:

1) Wow! What a question! My grandfather always said that your attitude will predict what you will do when in a spot. My attitude was always "wanting to do the best I could" with our staff.

Ken Knipper
Kentucky NVFC Director

2) As an old teacher of mine once said, "Do not let diarrhea of the mouth lead to constipation of the brain. Think before you act."

Chief Harry Carter, Ph.D. (Retired)
Adelphia, N.J. Fire Department

Think about the Thoughts You Think

Do not believe everything you think. Do not allow a bad case of the "What-ifs" to control you. Be very careful about what you say to yourself. Many of us load ourselves up with negative thinking. Our thinking impacts the quality of our leadership. Therefore, we must ask an important question: "What should our response be?"

This cavalier reaction will suggest that the answer lies within the removal of negative thoughts. Caution: Removed negative thoughts that are not replaced will re-surface. Therefore, the answer in relationship to the mandate (do not believe everything you think) has to do with the replacing, not merely the removal, of negative thoughts.

We suggest that it is too nebulous to seek to replace negative thoughts with positive thoughts. Negative thoughts must be replaced with thoughts of gratitude. Worded another way, gratitude need not be a back-end response. Gratitude can be a front end ignighter and rudder enabling you, the leader, to refuse to believe everything you think.

Gratitude wants to give you a way to transcend being caught or trapped by "What-if" thinking. Learn to view gratitude as a way to move beyond the trap of negative thinking. Value gratitude as ignighter, starter, initiator, sustainer, nurturer, and enabler. Think beyond – "Something wonderful happens and I am grateful." Think – "I am grateful and something wonderful happens. I am grateful and I am not believing my negative thoughts as much."

Be Grateful for:

- Moments when excessive, negative "What-if" thinking has less power over you,
- Moments when "What-if" thinking actually proves helpful (there are many such moments),
- The times you do not believe everything you think – your little victories,
- Your ability to evaluate,
- The capacity to change,
- The power to decide, implement, and nurture,
- The ability to modify,
- Your army of allies,
- Your arsenal of resources,
- Those who bring joy to your life,
- Your strengths,
- Spiritual strength.

Think of Gratitude as:

- Ammunition against excessive wasteland thinking,
- A substitute for extreme negativity,
- A back-end sensation,
- A front-end initiative,
- A reaction,
- A response,
- A personal appreciation,
- A personal motivator.

Your Mind: A Marvelous Mold and Hold Vessel

Do not believe everything you think! In the battle against excessive and negative "What-ifing," place gratitude into your quiver of response options. Leverage gratitude to work for you. Gratitude can bless you with resiliency in the midst of an onslaught of negativity. Your mind is a temple – a marvelous mold and hold vessel. Do not allow it to hold everything you think. Take care of yourself. Exercise gratitude.

****

"Did you ever stop to think, and forget to start again?"
-Winnie the Pooh

****

CHAPTER 10

Differentiating Leadership from Management

"Leadership and Management are not the same. On one hand you have successful methods of accomplishing tasks (management). On the other hand, you have the ability to fundamentally change attitudes and behavior (leadership)."

-Chief Rob Carnahan
Tualitan Valley, OR Fire/Rescue

"Go easy on the lectures; responsibility is a lot like love. It's better demonstrated than talked about. Show more and tell less."

-JMB

"Leadership is grounded in communication, process, and inspiration/influence. Management is rooted in control, event, and perhaps mere imposition"

-SMG

****

Leadership and management are not the same thing!

Quite frankly, it tires many – hearing others repeatedly refer to leadership and management as if they are the same thing. They are not the same thing. Unfortunately, many leaders act like managers and their teams suffer. This short chapter will highlight the difference between management and leadership.

Management

Management is control-centered, event-driven, and often leverages imposition. Management is not bad, but it is not leadership. It is not a necessary evil, it is a necessary function. Managers are needed. But leaders do not need to act like managers all of the time. When leaders forget to lead and only manage, team members are inclined to quit, or actually quit before they quit. Journeys are not serviced.

Leaders wear different focus-lights than managers. They are both important! This in no way implies that managers do not make huge differences! They do!! Managers need to be managers and leaders need to be leaders. On occasion, one person will have to wear the managerial hat and the leadership hat.

****

"Management is controlling the task at hand. Leadership is having division and motivation. It is being willing to create change and improvements."

-Chief Michael VanZile
Auburn, IN Fire Dept

****

Leadership

Leadership is people-centered, communication-driven, and often utilizes inspiration. Authentic leaders not only see the people out there, they service their journeys. In many instances, leaders are people-centered to the degree that they want each team member to claim ownership in the inventory of growth-ideas before those ideas materialize.

Authentic leaders ground themselves in communication – recognizing and validating the five elements of communication: source, message, channel, receiver, perception. Genuine leaders retreat from imposition and bring to task inspiration. They recognize that leadership is more about influence than power and more about people than position. In a broad sense, leaders recognize that they work with other leaders.

Ultimately, each person who works with you can be perceived as a leader – influencing, inspiring, communicating. Although there are *Uppercase* and *lowercase leaders*, leadership is too grand to limit it to so few.

There is a leader within you. Do not confuse management with leadership!

Never Say

There are several words and phrases that leaders avoid. Authentic leaders never use the term "subordinate." They refer to team members as working "with" them not "for" them. They shy away from "constructive criticism" and use the term "feedback."

****

"You lead people; you manage things."
-Ty Dickerson

****

Think Communication, Not Control

What do they see when they see you leading? When leaders think like managers, control is emphasized more than communication. If your team members think "control" when they see you coming and not "communication," then, you have some work to do. Begin your work by acting like a leader, not a manager.

Leadership, at its best, opens doors. It does not close doors of opportunity. When "control" is your mantra, you are limiting, not enabling, your team members. Being open to "input from others" does not mean you do not have preferences as to idea and approach. Openness will not always equal agreement or acquiescence. There will certainly be times when you have to say "no" to them and "yes" to your leadership-intuition.

When your team members see you coming, you want them to think "leader" not "manager." The key lies within their perception of you. How they perceive you is critical! Perception will be addressed further in subsequent chapters of *Lessons Learned*.

Leadership Is Reciprocal

Both of us spend many days speaking to delightful audiences. Upon conclusion, we are often asked: "Where do you get your energy?" Stephen will respond, "From ya'll." John being more diplomatic, will express, "The energy I send out to the audience comes back to me from the audience."

Leadership extended invites leadership returned. Act like a manager, you are likely to produce managers. Act like a leaders, you are likely to produce leaders. Managers and leaders seem to operate within a different time frame. Managers think in terms of event; leaders think in terms of process.

Yes!

Yes. There is a significant difference between leadership and management. This difference is being detected more as the years pass. This is a good thing for you and for those you lead.

****

"Leaders take the step to have others manage daily tasks, while showing them examples of leadership – compassion, trust, follow-through, walking-the-talk."

-Chief Jim Grady, III
Frankfort, IL Fire District

****

CHAPTER 11

Motivating the Self

"You need to be positive about yourself to be a positive leader. There is a fine line between confidence and arrogance, but being a positive and confident person will make you a positive and confident leader."

-Chief Michael VanZile
Auburn, IN Fire Dept.

"Motivating the self is about re-learning as much as it is about learning."

-JMB

"Sitting around, waiting for happy endings will not create motivation. There comes a moment when each of us must exclaim: 'If there is to be action, I must take action.'"

-SMG

****

Motivation is an inside work. No one can do your motivation-labor for you. Motivation is centered in choice - grounded in the choices you make. Your choices fuel your motivation.

Basketball Hall of Famer (1993) Bill Walton touched on the core of motivating the self when he described Coach John Wooden (for whom he played while at UCLA). Bill Walton's sentiments are echoed by a legion of Wooden's players, fans, and friends.

****

> John Wooden represents the conquest of substance over height, the triumph of achievement over erratic flailing, the conquest of discipline over gambling, and the triumph of executing an organized plan over hoping that you'll be lucky, hot, or in the zone. John Wooden also represents the conquest of sacrifice, hard work, and commitment to achievement over the pipe dream that someone will give you something or that you can take a pill or turn a key to get what you want.
>
> -Bill Walton

****

Ways to Motivate Yourself

Earlier in *Lessons Learned*, we addressed the importance of servicing your journey. One of your fundamental responsibilities is to keep yourself motivated. We continue this chapter by listing several ways to motivate yourself.

Define Your Dream

Avoid the land of ambiguity and confusing. Listen to your passion. Name and sculpt your dream by allowing your interests and talents to serve as a rudder for dream definition. Flex. Seek His help through prayer. Play to your strengths. Be specific when naming your dream.

Select "Start a landscape business" over "Go into business for myself." Choose "Write romance novels" over "Become an author." Decide to "Become a world renowned pianist" rather than "Go into music." Choose to "Pursue computer animation" over "Study art."

****

"You'll be as happy as you make up your mind to be."
-Abraham Lincoln

****

See Your Dream Happening!

Harness the wonderful image your mind's eye is preparing for you. Visualize your dream bursting into life and confidently marching toward maturity. Give your dream every benefit of doubt you can muster on its behalf. View in your head and heart the way your world will look once you reach dream-accomplishment.

Expect and Ignite

Give your defined and visualized dream a wake-up call. Enhance your passion with an enthusiastic dream-commencement. Call in your "friend-force." Gift yourself and your dream with the inertia that an authentic and competent cadre of supporters has to offer. Excite your force of friends. Then receive a spark from them that will help your dream ignite and catch fire.

Enjoy and Expect

Enjoy the flow. Expect some detours. With a dream in focus, with clarity of purpose at your side, you are ready for pursuit. You have every right to be excited about the journey and the dream. Stack the odds for success in your favor by orchestrating the journey so that it equals what you will enjoy, rather than what you will endure. Prepare for enjoyment, but also expect that at least occasionally you will travel by detour. Anticipate some detours. Deny the detours any opportunity to rob you of your joy.

Seize Your Opportunities

Warning: Postponement-pouches will be everywhere. Watch out for them. Procrastination will wear camouflage. When appropriate opportunities for advancement of your dream objective appear, leap for them. Do not analyze them to death. Swallow them whole. Be very leery of opportunity-evaporation.

Monitor Your Thoughts

Think about the thoughts you think. Remember that the thoughts you think impact the dreams you design. Discard your negative thoughts in the dump. Do not allow them to trash your dream. Deposit your positive thoughts of gratitude in the bank. Keep your positive thoughts around, so they can continue to service your journey. Relate to your "thought-life factor" as either a dream discourager or as a dream encourager, either a dream breaker or a dream maker.

Bring Home the Dream

Finish what you started. Bring the dream-journey to a point of arrival. Reach the destination. Touch "finished-ness." Share the accomplishment with supportive team members and with friends. The completion and the sharing will prepare you for the final rule.

Celebrate the Cycle

Ultimately, the realization of a dream does not equal an ending. It more closely resembles another beginning. Accomplishment gives way to anticipation. Finished-ness invites the future. There is a hoisting of a huge flag that states, with unabashed affirmation, "The best is yet to be."

Closing the gap between having a dream and pursuing a dream will be facilitated when you brace yourself with the preceding steps!

****

"Success leaves clues...and so does failure."

-Chief Raul A. Angulo
Seattle, WA Fire Department

****

CHAPTER 12

Creating a Motivational Environment

"Good leaders work themselves out of a job. They do this by developing and preparing those potential leaders under their command to take their place. Any leader who has selfishly made themselves "indispensable" has done the greatest disservice to their organization and their team members, they have set the stage for eventual failure."

-Joseph E. Waiscott
Director of Training
IN Dept of Homeland Security

"We teach our firefighters in three ways:
1) The first is by example.
2) The second is by example.
3) The third is by example.
If your firefighters should not be doing it, neither should you."

-JMB

"We make a huge mistake when we suggest to them that their growth is dependent upon 'a motivator.' Their growth is dependent upon their choices. The best we can do is to create a motivational environment where they become more likely to choose to motivate themselves."

-SMG

****

The motivation-button resides on the inside, not on the outside. As you think about lessons you might learn about leadership, think in two's: 1) Motivate yourself; 2) Create a motivational environment where others are more likely to motivate themselves.

Remember that "service" is a verb. Your high challenge as a leader is to service the journey of your team members. Create and maintain a motivational environment for team members.

Influence is not an opportunity of a select few. Influence is your opportunity.

Re-think "external motivation!" Think "creating a motivational environment!" Think of your leadership as influence, not imposition. Think of your leadership as inspiration, not as button-pushing.

Our Respondents Have It Right

1) I ensure a non-hostile, open environment for dealing with day-to-day issues. I *encourage* all officers to treat each other with respect. Firefighters must have confidence in open communication and behavioral standards that apply to everyone. Assurance that *Uppercase leaders* are doing everything possible to support *lowercase leaders* is essential in creating a motivational environment. Very simply, as the Chief of the Department, I actually work for them, as opposed to them working for me.

Chief Stephen R. M. Moreno, III
Tarpon Springs, FL Fire Rescue

2) I create a motivational environment by giving our team members the opportunity to provide input and guidance in their own outcome. I give them recognition for their accomplishments.

Chief Raymond S. Clark (Retired)
Bernalillo County, NM Fire and Rescue

3) The answer to the creation of a motivational environment is to be positive. We exploit the things we do right. We let personnel know that it is OK to make mistakes for improvement.

Assistant Fire Chief Jim Morgan
Casa Grande, AZ Fire Department

4) I ask them what it is they want to do. I see whether there is a way to make it possible for that to happen in a harmonious way with the goals of the organization.

Chief George Good
Tolleson, AZ Fire Department

Clues along Your Way

The traits you relish in others, traits that crafted their influence upon your life, should signal to you traits that will help you influence your team members. You will be most effective in creating a motivational environment when you replicate what was so meaningful to you.

Think of that scout master, the Sunday School teacher, the parent or grandparent, or friend who exemplified traits that created a motivational environment for you. I suspect you will think of the following:

Loyalty: They did not disconnect on a whim. Their support was not fickled.

Courage: They cared enough to confront. Their courage came out of love.

Affirmation: They were specific and intense when they affirmed you.

Grounded: They did not shake easily. They were well rooted.

Flexible: They were willing to re-think about it.

Open: They gave you a chance – even to make a mistake.

The Power of Praise

Praise will help you create a motivational environment. But you must be very careful here. The power of praise is diluted, and perhaps even negated, unless it passes the SAS test. Praise must be Specific, Appropriate, and Selective.

The Enemy of Specificity Is Generalization

Do not say, "Good Job on that speech." Say, "You did a good job *because* you paid the preparation price, you organized your thoughts well, and you used clean humor. You also had good eye contact. Most importantly, you were real."

As you seek to create a motivational environment, remember that you work with insecure partners. We are all insecure. An insecure partner will compare the intensity and specificity of your 'statements of confrontation' to the intensity and specificity to your 'statements of affirmation.'

The Enemy of Appropriateness Is Out-of-Line

Inappropriate praise is out-of-line with the creation of a motivational environment. Do not praise a team captain when it is the team that did the work. That genre of praise will backfire. Be sure the praise you send out is merited.

The Enemy of Selectivity Is Overuse

The creation of a motivational environment will be impeded if you are persistently praising and rarely caring enough to confront. The over-done does not equal the well done; it equals the poorly done.

****

"He who praises everybody, praises nobody."
-Samuel Johnson

****

The Power of Example

A thread that binds the fabric of the study was the awareness of the power of example in leadership. Void example, a motivational environment will not be created. Your expectation minus your example will equal exasperation on the part of your team members.

At the risk of re-stating, let us address the danger of seeking to give what you do not have. You cannot exemplify what you want to exemplify if you refuse to service your own journey.

There is an exciting shifting taking place within leadership circles. The relationship between servicing the journey of oneself and servicing the journey of the team is becoming more obvious.

Creation Is Process

As you seek to craft a motivational environment within your team, celebrate incremental "finished-ness." If you wait until the team is fully motivated to celebrate any progress, your waiting will begin to equal eternal frustration.

Many of our respondents have been at this for decades and they will be the first to state: "When the issue is the creation of a motivational environment, I have not yet arrived." Bring to task the power of praise, the power of example, and the potency of patience.

Caution: Avoid Assumption

I like to tell this story to emphasize the powerful danger of assumption when you are trying to create a motivational environment.

The setting was Istanbul, Turkey. I had just finished presenting for the Turkey Human Resource Conference and was heading back to the airport. The person riding with me, a conference attendee, inquired: "Mr. Gower, could you please explain to me why my boss always catches me doing wrong but never seems to catch me doing well?"

I responded: "I will be delighted to share an observation. I would like to begin by rephrasing your concern. I suspect your supervisor catches you doing wrong; and, I suspect he catches you doing well. The issue is not of 'catching' and 'non-catching,' I imagine the issue is not so much 'catching' as it is 'translating.' As I work with our clients, I often observe them 'catching and translating' when the issue is weakness-confrontation. However, at the point of strength-affirmation these same clients seem to 'catch' but not 'translate.'"

The question is this: If my analysis is correct, if we have a tendency to "catch and translate" at the point of weakness, but only "catch" at the point of strength, then why is that so? The answer lies in our tendency to assume. When we catch someone doing something wrong, our inclination is to express our feelings. When we catch someone doing something well, our tendency is to assume that they know what we know, know what we wish they knew, or know how we feel.

Assumption does not have as much power over us when we are mad, but it sure has a lot of power over us when we are glad. If we are to be authentic and effective as we seek to service the journey of our team members (and customers), we must learn to transcend assumption. The "how to" here is a two-fold: awareness and avoidance. 1) Be aware of your tendency to assume at the point of affirmation. 2) Avoid the tendency to assume.

If we have an attitude of difference (if we care about our team members) and do not act out our attitude, then our team members are most likely to perceive an attitude of indifference on our part. Remember: They do not respond to your attitude (the catching) – in fact, they probably do not even know your attitude. They respond to your action (the translating). Do not merely "catch" them doing well. When you "catch" them doing well, "translate." The attitude minus the action equals the aggravation.

It Will Not Happen over Night

The results of your creating a motivational environment for others may never be "apparent" to you. Perhaps it is more likely that it will be a "long time" before they do become apparent.

I appreciate the experience involving Coach Amos Alonzo Stagg while he was coaching at the University of Chicago. After a stellar year, a reporter exclaimed to the coach: "Coach Stagg, it was a great year! A really great year." Coach Stagg responded: "I won't know for another twenty years or so whether you are correct."

Coach John Wooden will share a similar sentiment. I prefer to read it often:

****

I'm asked, 'Coach, aren't you particularly proud of all of the players that went on to the pros after they left UCLA...?' Yes, but I am equally proud of the fellows that became doctors, lawyers, dentists, ministers, businessmen, teachers, and coaches.

-Coach John Wooden

****

Training: A Huge Part of the Creating

One of the games I used to play involved taking the letters within a word, or two or three words, and make other words from those letters. It was both fun and mentally stimulating.

When I look at the letters within "Creating a Motivational Environment," the first word I think of is "training." There is no struggle at this point. "Trains" just seems to jump out from the letters in "Creating a Motivational Environment." A chapter with this name on such an important subject cannot be addressed without visiting the issue of training.

Earlier in *Lessons Learned*, I used the phrase "service their journey." Within Fire-Rescue, there is absolutely no way to service a journey without grounding "the servicing" with a consistent emphasis on training.

****

"The creating of a motivational environment within Fire-Rescue mandates a heavy and consistent emphasis on training. The creation of such an environment is nothing but illusion minus a strong training-structure."

-SMG

****

No Breaks

Until 2003, I had never presented for Fire-Rescue, nor for law enforcement. Now, eighty percent of my presentations and small group leadership sessions are for Fire-Rescue and law enforcement.

Before 2003, I rarely took a break during my presentation. If I took a break, it was few.

This is certainly not the case with the Fire-Rescue and law enforcement audiences. Ordinarily, during each presentation, these participants expect at least one break per hour. However, when it comes to training, team members understand the seriousness of continuous training without taking a break.

The Scary Thing

When it comes to training, it is essential you ask the following questions: "Is it rememorable? Will this training remain within the head and the heart of the trainee?"

This much I know: On a national average, close to seventy-five percent of training evaporates within a week of taking place. At The Gower Group, Inc., I seek to better that figure through a seven step process:

1) I pay the preparation price. Preparation is grounded by a marriage between the group's needs or theme and my hard work.

2) My training is highly interactive.

3) On occasion, I remember that "serious training" can have a "light heartedness." When appropriate, humor offers much help.

4) I provide numerous methods to recapture the content: DVD/CD packs, books, reminder cards, and handouts.

5) During the presentation, I ask the participants to share what they have learned from the training.

6) I review the participants' evaluations. This allows me to sculpt strengths and chisel weaknesses.

7) I leave grateful for the priviledge of the platform - the honor to train.

Is It Rememorable?

Recently, I discovered within my Precious File a letter that I received more than a decade ago. To emphasize that the seven-step process previously listed works, I share a small portion of that letter.

> It has been almost a year since I've heard you speak . . . from the first week forward, I have seen indications that your presentation has had a profound and lasting effect. The impact has been powerful and pervasive . . . Stephen, the transfer of knowledge was much more complete than I thought possible.
>
> -Grady W. Brown
> Senior Vice President, Mattel
> El Segundo, CA

****

"The two keys to excellent content, high quality, and useful training are 'observable' and 'measurable.'"
-JMB

****

Involvement

Many of the respondents indicated a responsibility to remain involved at the core of their training. An example of such thinking is shared by Chief Angulo from the Seattle Fire Department.

****

> I am very involved in training. I really do try to make every day a training day. I really do believe 'train like your life depends on it...because it does!' 1) I try to make realistic, challenging drills. 2) I drill for technique and finesse. 3) I always include some obstacle or problem that the crew has to solve to be successful at the objective.
>
> -Chief Raul A. Angulo
> Seattle, WA Fire Department

****

Remember two things: 1) Your involvement at point of training can be helpful. 2) Training is definitely involved with creating a motivational environment.

Creating a Motivational Environment Is Not Easy

The task I have been addressing in this chapter of *Lessons Learned* is not a simple challenge. It is both complex and difficult. There is no doubt that the continuous toil is valid.

You Never Know

We never know when we are doing something that may have a huge impact on someone's life. One of the difference-makers in my life was Dr. Archie Sharretts from Toccoa, Georgia. Dr, Sharretts' was my high school band instructor.

At 10:00 on a Monday night, Dr. Sharretts called my mother and said: "India, we have a problem. You know that Stephen is a member of our marching band at Toccoa High School. Our band has fifty members, forty-nine of them can march; and then there is Stephen. I have tried everything imaginable and have found the solution that will give us the change we need. It will not bring embarrassment or frustration to Stephen. I believe he has a wonderful voice and an outgoing personality. I think he would serve well as our half-time announcer for the band."

Dr. Archie Sharretts gave me the opportunity and encouragement to speak in public. Now, after more than 5,000 presentations in forty-nine states and ten countries, I am still speaking in public.

What Dr. Sharretts could do with music - elicit harmony from discord, build symphony from more than a few sour notes, he did with me. Dr. Sharretts may not have given this move a second thought, but I have given it much thought. I am perpetually reminded that what one person thinks to be "insignificant" can prove to be very "significant."

****

"The difference you make in the lives
of others may well be camouflaged.
Just because you cannot see the differences
does not mean they are not there."
-SMG

****

CHAPTER 13

Taking a Strength Too Far

"My strength is a passion and enthusiasm for the job. My weakness is in the area of delegation. After eighteen years as a company officer, I still have a hard time learning to delegate."

-Chief Raul A. Angulo
Seattle, WA Fire Department

" Learning is a choice. The choice must always be grounded at the point of balance."

-JMB

"Enthusiasm can be a blessing; exaggeration can equal that which is extremely problematic."

-SMG

****

We Seemed to Touch a Button Here

In the survey, we shared a statement, then a question: "Struggle, a traveling by detour, even a mistake can teach lessons. What have you learned from your 'where you have been?'"

Paragraphs were written by respondents to this question. An indication of the impact of this issue on the lives of leaders was addressed by one participant in this fashion: "I probably don't have enough space here."

Other more specific responses included the following:

1) "I am learning to be patient, nothing happens in the time we want it to. I am also learning to choose my team wisely. Finally, the lesson struggle has taught me is not to allow unacceptable behavior or performance to go on too long."

2) "I have learned to identify political subtitles in order to help avoid pitfalls."

3) "My 'where I have been' has taught me that communication is the key to everything. But, you have to find the correct door in which to use it."

4) "The lesson I have learned is that there are times when you have to confront. Confront, maintain your integrity, even if it hurts."

5) "I have learned that mistakes are an educational opportunity. The learning can be measured by how many times one commits the same mistake."

6) "I have made a mistake in the area of 'respect.' I demanded respect as a new officer. I forgot that respect must be earned. I pitched a 'temper-tantrum' because my authority had been challenged. The experience set me back six months, but taught me a very important lesson. My eyes were open to not only the cause of my early failure at leadership, but the very root cause for the failures of many. A white shirt and gold bugles do not a leader make."

7) "The biggest mistake I ever made occurred many years ago when I was a Captain. I sounded off about an idea a Chief had. I stated that I thought it was stupid. I was pulled aside by my Battalion Chief and told never to do that again. I learned not to place doubt in the minds of others about the leadership of their Chiefs."

****

"You should always be asking yourself a very important question: 'Am I learning from my mistakes?'"
-JMB

****

From Generalization to Specificity

The first part of this chapter has been centered on mistakes in general. We were grateful for the survey-responses that indicated a courage and a boldness at this point.

A study of the surveys indicated, in many cases, a linkage between a particular strength and a weakness. There was a "related-ness" between the two because the weakness was actually a strength taken too far.

Examples of Strengths Taken Too Far

Many of us have a friend who incessantly mentions our name while we are with him. Now he is a fine man and means well – having been trained that his customers appreciate hearing their name. The reference to a person's name, while having a conversation with that person, can prove beneficial in a plethora of scenarios. However, this friend might be taking the strength of "speaking on a first name basis" too far – so far that he actually appears contrived, routine, rhythmic, and programmed to a fault.

The example of mentioning another's name, so frequently that it not only appears aggravating, but also irritating, and problematic, does not stand alone. Some other examples of strengths taken too far are addressed below. Perhaps you can identify with one of the pictures these words will paint:

1) Authority is essential. There comes a time for firmness and decisiveness. Authority taken too far can equal an abrasive attitude that stifles initiative and frightens, rather than encourages, team members.

2) Friendship between a supervisor and a team member can establish trust and loyalty. Yet, when a supervisor takes friendship "too far," he can lose the capacity to be objective. Friendship taken too far can equal an exaggerated emphasis on affirmation and a timidity or reluctance when it comes to caring enough to confront.

3) Eye contact is essential if you are addressing one team member, or hundreds in an audience. Your nervous energy about speaking in public can work for you, rather than against you, when you establish eye contact with your audience. Eye contact can help create a beneficial connection. However, eye contact taken "too far" can result in a "perceived staring down" that can equal intimidation, imposition, and embarrassment.

4) Humor can serve as an elixir that calms an uptight audience. Clean humor can serve as a hinge that opens the door to a particular point you are seeking to emphasize. Taken too far, humor can approach a teasing that becomes a torture.

5) Organization managed well can create a structure for action, a method of approach, a model of explanation. Organization taken "too far" can crimp response, postpone decisiveness or paralyze performance.

6) Vulnerability can birth a perceived humanness, a refreshing openness, a striking courage, and even humility. Vulnerability taken "too far" can violate any purity of motive as it begins to resemble manipulation.

7) Familiarity with your presentation will communicate to your audience that you have paid the preparation price. You are so familiar with your content that you control any notes you might be using; your notes do not control you. Familiarity with your presentation will allow you "flex" room when distractions unfold. Familiarity taken "too far" can equal a perceived "memorized" presentation rather than a perceived "learned" presentation. When familiarity begins to equal memorization, effectiveness will dwindle – you will appear contrived, cold, routine, distanced, and as if you are merely going through the motions. The form (with which you are so familiar) minus the force (absent because you have taken familiarity "too far") can equal a farce (a horrid void of authenticity).

8) Dedication to the work phase of your life can touch points of satisfaction and maximize performance. Dedication to the work phase of your life taken "too far" can impact, in a negative fashion, your responsibility to service the journeys of family, friends, and self. The work phase of your life is an important extension of your life (not separate from your life). But when you emphasize work, at the expense of important relationships, you run the risk of negatively impacting those relationships.

****

"The statement, 'work-life-balance' does not make sense. While you are working, your life is going on. However, 'work-family-balance' and 'work-leisure-balance' do make sense."
-SMG

****

9) Spontaneity, grounded in pleasant surprises, can equal stellar refreshment. Some of our best ideas emerge as a natural inclination or an unconstrained behavior. We do not grab these ideas, these ideas grab us, without a hint of external provocation. Spontaneity taken too far can equal an impulsiveness void of any discernment – both raw and rude.

10) Honesty, a trait that flows out from internal mandates that value truth, sincerity, and authenticity, is expected in professional and personal circles. Honesty can be taken "too far" as to equal: a) a naïveté that is blinding,

and b) a harshness that results (unnecessarily) from true words that quite simply should not have been said.

11) Sensitivity is a virtue that can bless your team members and your family. When others detect that you are sensitive about their feelings, professional and personal relationships profit. My experience is that there is a back-side to sensitivity. Often, those who are appropriately sensitive toward others can be inappropriately too sensitive about ourselves. Sensitivity taken "too far" can equal a self-absorption that results in a paranoia.

Two Important Exceptions

Any wrap-up of our time addressing strengths taken too far must include the exceptions to the rule: integrity and safety. Ultimately, there is no "extreme" when the issue is basic integrity. If integrity equals a complete correspondence with one's appropriate internal mandates, then it is difficult to place limits upon it. Emphasis on safety is critical.

****

"Never let safety take a shift off."
-Chief Dan Jones
Chapel Hill, NC

****

Balance Is the Goal

A strength taken "too far" is a challenge for each of us. We must recognize that extremes can prove problematic. Balance is the goal. Discernment and restraint are roads that lead to the goal. The key toward discernment and restraint stands on two legs: awareness of a tendency to take a strength too far and avoiding the temptation to overextend a strength.

****

"Happiness is not a matter of intensity but of balance, order, rhythm and harmony."
-Thomas Merton

****

CHAPTER 14

How They Perceive You Is Your Business

"Perception and leadership go hand in hand."
-Chief Robert Rielage
Moscow, OH Fire Dept.

"Perception creates a vital link with team members, especially during adverse times."
-JMB

"One of the most important questions you can ask is 'what do they see when they see me coming?"
-SMG

****

Ask many people what my middle name is and they will be inclined to answer: "Perception." For more than a quarter of a century, I have studied communication and leadership. It is my conviction that the mistake most of us make is that we do not factor into our communication and leadership equations the power of perception.

I have written two books on this subject: *What Do They See When They See You Coming? The Power of Perception over Reality* and *Perception: Make It Your Business*. Over the years, I have learned how to condense the core of these two books into what I refer to as "The Five Mega Truths of Perception."

The bulk of this chapter will briefly address each of these critical elements of perception. I invite you to take them very seriously. You cannot claim and polish the leader and follower within you without asking the perception-question: What do they see when they see me coming?

The Microphone

Your microphone is always on! It is particularly alive when you are tired, angry, frustrated, in the midst of partying, or after you have partied. Remember you are always sending out messages. In this sense, you are never off duty.

Starting Point/Pace

Our team members do not have the same starting points, nor do we run/learn at the same pace! Our experiences, strengths, weaknesses, and attitudes are as different from each other as are our unique personalities. Unfortunately, our tendency is to forget or ignore this reality, and thus assume that we are similar at point of start and pace.

The Enigma of Language

We do not speak the same language, even if we all speak English. The idea that a word or phrase means the same thing to everyone is a huge mis-conception. What someone says and what you hear can be very different.

For purposes of re-statement, let me emphasize the following points: 1) The conjunction "with" as in "they work with me" is superior to the conjunction "for" as in "they work for me." 2) The word "feedback" is superior to the word "criticism." You can share with me: "Stephen, I would like to offer you 'some constructive criticism.'" You will be saying three words, I will hear one word - "criticism." 3) A word that should never be used is "subordinate."

Remember: What you mean to say and what they hear can be very different - even if both of you speak English.

The Thatch Hut

Perception is driven by the perceiver—from underneath a "Thatch Hut!" Past experiences and perspectives determine, to a large degree, what others see when they see you coming. Thatch huts rule. Thatch is much more than an accumulation of mown fescue that hangs around on the ground - harming the growth of the grass. Thatch is the accumulation of their experiences that determines their perception.

A Tale of Thatch

I am a tale of thatch.
In my heart, I wear a patch.
If you wonder what it's like to be like me,
You must first consider what I see.

What I see depends on what I've seen.
Where I am relates to where I've been.
My past hurt is still my major thrusts.
My patch holds firm until I trust.

Please come visit my Thatch Hut.
I do not wish that we stay in a rut.
Perhaps if you discover what I see,
Then together we can be all we are meant to be.

-Stephen M. Gower, CSP
From *What Do They See When They See You Coming?*
Copyright © 1993.

****

"Perception is in the beholder's eye."
-Chief Patrick Laurienti
N. Washington Fire Protection
Denver, CO

****

The Mystery of Significance

What is insignificant to you can be extremely significant to someone else! What you say and do can cause a reaction from another that is much stronger than you expected. In reality, you are precipitating or triggering the "shifting back" of another - perhaps leading them to go back to an uncomfortable experience. That uncomfortable experience still holds power over them, transitioning what you perceive as insignificant into what they perceive as significant.

****

"Some contend that perception is reality.
I disagree. I can perceive the chair I am sitting
in as a stool. That does not make it a stool.
But, when it comes to relationships,
perception may actually be more
powerful than reality."
-SMG

****

The Relationship between Perception and Communication

In Chapter Five of *Lessons Learned,* I addressed the 9C's behind personal excellence (Character, Competency, Confidence, Compassion, Commitment, Credibility, Courage, Concentration, and Classification). In this chapter, there is the "tenth C" that we briefly referred to in Chapter Five. The relationship between perception and communication is significant enough for special attention.

Four Is One Too Few

Traditionally, we are taught, that communication is limited to four elements: Source, Message, Channel, and Receiver. Upon further reflection, I have become convinced that there is a fifth element. Before that particular element is addressed, an understanding of the first four elements will be helpful.

Source

The one who sends the data, or starts the process of communication is considered the source. To use this book as an example, I am the source of communication (with the help of Chief John M. Buckman, III, IAFC President 2001-2002).

It will also be helpful to think of the source of communication as the initiator of thought. You could also think of the source of communication as the point person, the starting pitcher, or as the man who utters: "Gentlemen, start your engines."

Message

The message is the substance of the communication. It is the core of the data that is being expressed.

In the case of this book, the message is: *Lessons Learned from Fire-Rescue Leaders.* The message is the heart of what is being communicated.

Channel

One cannot pursue personal excellence, or understand perception, without appreciating the concept of "channel." To value "channel" is to set the stage for elements four and five.

The "channel" is the manner in which the message is moving from the source to the receiver. In the case of this book, I (source) am sending a concept (message) in a certain way. That "way" equals the "channel."

For purposes of this book, the channel is the written word. What must be comprehended, as one explores the phenomenon of perception is that there are a plethora of channels: the written word, the spoken word, sign language, smoke signals, morse code, braille, and body language. The channel will influence the way the receiver perceives your message.

Receiver

In football, the quarterback passes the ball to the receiver. In communication, the source passes the message, by way of a particular channel, to the receiver.

In the case of this book, you are receiving from me a message that travels by way of the written language. A hint that will eventually lead us to element number five in communication is this fact: "If thousands of different receivers read this book, what one receiver interprets as the core may not equal what other persons perceive is the core of the message."

Perception Is the Fifth Element

The communication-failure that is exhibited by many communicators and by many leaders is simple but very important. This failure is grounded in assumption. We are assuming that information flows from source to receiver in an "un-filtered fashion." This has been addressed earlier but is important enough to mandate re-statement.

"What you say" and "what I hear" may not be the same thing. As addressed in the "Thatch Hut" concept, perception is driven by the perceiver from underneath their "Thatch Hut."

The error that many of us exhibit is the failure to factor perception into our leadership and communication equations. There is more to communication than source, message, channel, and receiver. The fifth element of communication is perception.

****

"How they perceive you is your business."
-SMG

****

CHAPTER 15

Retirement Re-Think

"Many are coming to the fire service as a second career. Quite a number of these persons are from the military. This is extremely helpful for us. Although they may work a shorter period of time, they bring to task a tremendous amount of experience."

-Assistant Chief Matt Love
Woodmen Valley, Fire Dept.
Colorado Springs, CO

"The reality of a second career, both into and out from fire service,is not mere happenstance. It is becoming a regular occurrence."

-JMB

"I have considered it an enigma for decades - why many retire at the peak of their experience. This trend is changing. Many are re-thinking retirement and returning to work, perhaps in a different field and in an area that demands less time."

-SMG

****

This is the shortest chapter in *Lessons Learned.* For many of you, it may prove to be the most important chapter. Do not allow its brevity to imply any degree of insignificance.

The paragraphs that follow will address a major shifting. There is a radical re-direction of thinking toward the subject of retirement.

Retirement Is Not What It Used to Be

There are several reasons that justify a major re-thinking of the issue of retirement in our country: 1) We are living longer. 2) Working, perhaps in a second career, is a financial necessity. 3) As retirements, in certain fields in particular, require twenty years rather than thirty years of work, there is a natural inclination toward a second career. 4) The number of people who feel, along with me, that retirement at the peak of experience mandates a second thought is legion.

More, Not Less

Our time spent with Fire-Rescue leaders indicate that they are re-thinking retirement to a greater degree than the mass of society. Transition into a second career, either out from or into Fire and Rescue, is occurring more, not less.

Ready Begins with R-E-A-D

For purposes of emphasis, I mention again the importance of reading. Reading is supported with three specific books that you will find in the Recommended Reading list. To wet your appetite I will list and briefly describe these three books.

- *Avoid Retirement and Stay Alive* by David Bogan and Keith Davies (2008). The directness of the title continues throughout the book. A central question that is posed within the pages of this work is: "Why on earth are you worrying about retirement?" For many, the content of this book will be difficult to swallow. The authors are bold in their invitation: "Turn everything you have been conditioned to think about retirement on its head." Carrying a published date of 2008, this book brings an up-to-date perspective to the subject.

- *Re-working Retirement: A Practical Guide for Retirees Returning to Work* by Allyn I. Freeman and Robert E. Gorman (2008). Emphasizing the opportunity to do a job you "want" to rather than one you "have" to is a central theme of this book. There are helpful stories from other retirees returning to the workforce as well as a comprehensive reference guide for post-retirement employment. Carrying a published date of 2008, this work is also up-to-date in nature.

- *The New Professional Person's Retirement Lifestyle* by Jefferey Webber (2006). Broader in scope than the two previous books listed, this book addresses a broad spectrum of retirement options. Its central question is: "What do you do with all of that time?" I found pages 282 through 318 to be remarkably comprehensive. Within this section, you will find: 1) A four page bibliography, 2) a twenty-seven page website directory, and 3) a suggested reading section.

On Re-Thinking

Our tendency is to believe that thinking is related to "coming up with different answers." This chapter underscores re-thinking with the suggestion that we might consider asking different questions - moving from "When can I retire?" to "How can I re-think retirement and work, perhaps in a different way?"

****

"Live long and prosper."
-Mr. Spock
Star Trek
Series & Movies

****

CHAPTER 16

From Me to You

I am not sure why. It has been a struggle of mine for almost half a century. I can say, "Hello" with ease. I am a professional speaker, yet, I have a tendency to stutter when it is time to say "goodbye." "Goodbyes" come hard for me. But, as we say in the deep south "The time is nigh."

Before we approach our last page together, I want to thank our team at The Gower Group, Inc. They have visited this challenge with intensity at the point of this project, and with patience at the point of dealing with me.

My sincere thanks to Chief John M. Buckman, III. I have been the beneficiary of his insight and friendship. In that same vein, I express my gratitude to the Fire-Rescue professionals across the country who have blessed *Lessons Learned* with much authenticity and credibility.

Thank you for being interested. I would not be writing so many books if readers were not interested in the subjects I address. Your interest enables me to continue doing what I love to do. Expanding upon the gift you have given me, one of my greatest joys in life is writing. I cannot describe it. It is as if peace catches me by pleasant surprise. I rarely feel as free, calm, and creative as when I am writing.

Your reading this book whispers words of encouragement to me. Thank you for gifting me with the opportunity to do what I love.

I wish for you the same! Go lead, follow, enjoy!

-Stephen M. Gower, CSP
Spring 2008

Recommended Reading

(Note: Although a few of these books were written many years ago, we have made a concerted effort to research recently written data that will prove helpful. You will notice that most of these books carry a published date of 2007 or 2008.)

Bogan, David and Keith Davies. *Avoid Retirement and Stay Alive - The New Retirement Revolution.* New York: McGraw Hill, 2008.

Checketts, Darby. *Positive Conflict Transforms Opposition into Innovation.* Franklin Lakes, NJ: Career Press, 2007.

Compton, Dennis. *The Mental Aspects of Performance for Firefighters and Fire Officers*. Stillwater, OK: Fire Protection Publications, Oklahoma State University, 2004.

Compton, Dennis. *When in Doubt, Lead. Stillwater, OK: Fire Protection Publications*, Oklahoma State University, 1999.

Compton, Dennis. *When in Doubt, Lead...Part Two.* Stillwater, OK: Fire Protection Publications, Oklahoma State University, 2000.

Compton, Dennis. *When in Doubt, Lead...Part Three.* Stillwater, OK: Fire Protection Publications, Oklahoma State University, 2002.

Recommended Reading

Covey, Steven M. R. with Rebecca R. Merrill. *The Speed of Trust - The One Thing That Changes Everything*. New York: Free Press, 2006.

Dilenschneider, Robert L. Power and Influence - *The Rules Have Changed.* New York: McGraw Hill, 2007.

Dulworth, Michael. *The Connect Affect - Building Strong Personal, Professional, Virtual Networks*. San Francisco: Berrett-Koehler, 2008.

Eikenberry, Kevin. *Remarkable Leadership – Unleashing Your Leadership Potential One Skill at a Time.* San Francisco: Josey-Bass, 2007.

Farr, Michael and Laurence Shafkin, Ph.D. *150 Best Jobs for Your Skills*. Indianapolis: Jist, 2008.

Frankel, Lois P. *See Jane Lead - 99 Ways for Women to Take Charge at Work.* New York: Warner Business Books, 2007.

Freeman, Allyn I. and Robert E. Gorman. *A Practical Guide for Retirees Returning to the Workplace.* Avon, MA: Adams Business, 2008.

Gallo, Carmine. *Fire Them Up*. Hoboken, NJ: John Wiley and Sons, 2007.

Gower, Stephen M. *The Focus Crisis*. Toccoa: Lectern Publishing, 2008.

Gower, Stephen M. *Leadership Re-Think - How to Claim and Polish the Leader Within You.* Toccoa: Lectern Publishing, 2007.

Gower, Stephen M. *Stretchability! How to Build Your Agenda for Growth.* Toccoa: Lectern Publishing, 2008.

Gower, Stephen M. *What Do They See When They See You Coming?* Toccoa: Lectern Publishing, 1993.

Hansel, Tim. *When I Relax I Feel Guilty.* Elgin, IL: David C. Cook, 1979.

Hansel, Tim. *You Gotta Keep Dancin.'* Elgin, IL: David C. Cook, 1985.

Harkavy, Daniel. *Becoming a Coaching Leader.* Nashville: Thomas Nelson, 2007.

Hathaway, George. *Leadership Secrets from the Executive Office.* New York: MJF Books, 2004.

Heller, Robert. *Learning to Lead.* New York: DK Publishing, 1999.

Kellerman, Barbara. *Followership - How Followers Are Creating Change and Changing Leaders.* Boston: Harvard Business Press, 2008.

Knaus, William J. *Do It Now - Break the Procrastination Habit.* New York: John Wiley and Sons, 1998.

Recommended Reading

Loflin, Jones and Todd Mosig. *Juggling Elephants - An Easier Way to Get Your Most Important Things Done Now!* New York: Portfolio, 2007.

Logan, Dave and John King and Halee Fischer-Wright. *Tribal Leadership - Leveraging Natural Groups to Build a Thriving Organization.* New York: Harper Collins, 2008.

Martin, Roger. *The Opposable Mind - How Successful Leaders Win Through Integrative Thinking.* Boston: Harvard Business School, 2007.

Maxwell, John C. *Be a People Person - Effective Leadership Through Effective Relationships.* Colorado Springs: David C. Cook, 2007.

Maxwell, John C. *Be All You Can Be - A Challenge to Stretch Your God Govern Potential.* Colorado Springs: David C. Cook, 2007.

Maxwell, John C. *Developing the Leader Within You.* Nashville: Thomas Nelson Publishers, 1993.

Maxwell, John C. *Leadership Gold.* Nashville: Thomas Nelson, 2008.

Norville, Debra. *Thank You Power.* Nashville: Thomas Nelson, 2007.

Palmer, Russel E. *Ultimate Leadership - Winning Execution Strategies for Your Situation*. Upper Saddle River, NJ: Wharton School of Publishing, 2008.

Parker, James F. *Do the Right Thing*. Upper Saddle River, NJ: Wharton School Publishing, 2008.

Patterson, Karry and Joseph Grenny, David Mayfield, Ron McMillan, and Al Switzler. *Influencer - The Power to Change Anything*. New York: McGraw Hill, 2008.

Pogorzelski, Steve and Jesse Harriott, Ph.D. with Doug Hardy. *Finding Keepers - The Monsters Guide to Hiring and Holding the World's Best Employers*. New York: McGraw Hill, 2008.

Pratt, David (Compiled by). *The Impossible Takes Longer - The 1,000 Wisest Things Ever Said By Nobel Prize Laureates*. New York: Walker & Company, 2007.

Rath, Tom and Donald O. Clifton, Ph.D. *How Full Is Your Bucket? Positive Strategies for Work and Life*. New York: Gallup Press, 2004.

Rath, Tom. *Strengths Finder 2.0*. New York: Gallup Press, 2007.

Reichheld, Frederick, F. *The Loyalty Effect*. Boston: Harvard Business School Press, 1996.

Rohn, Jim. *Leading an Inspired Life.* United States of America: Nightingale-Conant Corp. 1997.

Sanborn, Mark. *You Don't Need a Title to be a Leader.* New York: Double Day, 2006.

Sanders, Tim. *The Likability Factor.* New York: Three Rivers Press, 2005.

Sherman, Doug and William Hendricks. *Your Work Matters to God.* Colorado Springs: Navpress, 1988.

Skomal, Lenore. *Gratitude.* Kennebunkport: Cider Mill Press Book Publishers, 2006.

Strock, James M. *Theodore Roosevelt on Leadership.* New York: Prima Publishing, 2001.

Tichy, Noel M. and Warren G. Bennis. *Judgment - How Winning Leaders Make Great Calls.* New York: Portfolio, 2007.

Tracy, Brian. *Flight Plan - The Real Secret of Success.* San Francisco: Berret-Koehler Publishers, Inc, 2008.

Webber, Jeffrey. *The New Professional Person's Retirement Lifestyle.* United States of America, Booklocker.com, 2006.

Recommended Reading

Windisch, Fred and Fred Crosby. *A Leadership Guide for Combination Fire Departments*. Boston: Jones and Brothers, 2007.

Wooden, John and Jay Carty. *One-On-One: Inspiring Conversations on Purpose, Passion, and the Pursuit of Success*. Ventura, CA: Regal Books, 2003.

Wooden, John and Steve Jamison. *Wooden - A Lifetime of Lessons on Leaders and Leadership*. New York: McGraw-Hill Publishers, 2007.

Wooden, Coach John, with Steve Jamison. *Wooden - A Lifetime of Observations and Reflections On and Off the Court*. Chicago: Contemporary Books, 1997.

Wooden, John and Steve Jamison. *Wooden On Leadership*. New York: McGraw-Hill Publishers, 2005.

Wooden, John with Steve Jamison. *My Personal Best: Life Lessons from an All-American Journey*. New York: McGraw-Hill, 2004.

Wooden, John with Jack Tobin. *They Call Me Coach*. New York: McGraw Hill, 2004.

About Stephen

Worldwide, Stephen M. Gower, CSP, is respected as "The Perception Professional." He works with organizations who want to lead change. He brings to the forefront an exploration and celebration of the remarkable relationship between individual team member choices and stellar team performance patterns. His unique blend of enthusiasm, experience, and content produces stunning results at the point of the passion behind change. His *What Do They See When They See You Coming?* book is recognized as the signature work on perception across the globe.

Earning a bachelor's degree from Mercer University and his master's degree from Emory University, Stephen has given more than 5,000 presentations and is a best selling author of eighteen books.

Contact Us:

For information on Stephen's keynote speeches, workshops, consulting, and educational material.

smg@stephengower.com
800-242-7404

About John

John M. Buckman has served as Fire Chief of German Township Volunteer Fire Department in Evansville, Indiana since 1977. He served as President of the International Association of Fire Chiefs in 2001-2002; currently serving as Program Planning Committee Chair Fire-Rescue International. In 1994, he co-founded the Volunteer and Combination Officers Section. In 2003, President George W. Bush appointed John to the Department of Homeland Security, State, Tribal, and Local Advisory Group. In 2000, he was appointed to the America Burning Revisited Commission by President Bill Clinton. He is the co-author of the 3rd Edition of Recruiting, Training and, Maintaining Volunteer Firefighters. Chief Buckman was selected by Fire Chief Magazine in 1995 as Fire Chief of the Year. He has authored over 100 articles and presented in all 50 states and Canada. In May 2008, the IN Governor Daniels presented John with a Meritorious Service Award.

He serves on several national advisory boards including Fire Engineering Magazine and Fire Department Instructors Conference. He is a founding member of the executive committee for the National Fire Academy Alumni Association, where he has served as Secretary-Treasurer since 1998. In 2007, the IAFC VCOS created the "John M. Buckman, III Leadership Award," to honor a chief officer from a volunteer or combination department for leadership and dedication.

Contact Us:

For additional information regarding John's presentations and articles, contact him at:

jmbuckman@aol.com
812-963-9077

Made in the USA
Middletown, DE
01 August 2023